THE ODER-NEISSE LINE

A REAPPRAISAL UNDER INTERNATIONAL LAW

PHILLIP A. BÜHLER

EAST EUROPEAN MONOGRAPHS, BOULDER
DISTRIBUTED BY COLUMBIA UNIVERSITY PRESS, NEW YORK

1990

EAST EUROPEAN MONOGRAPHS NO. CCLXXVII

ISBN 0-88033-174-7
Library of Congress Catalog Card Number 89-81325

Printed in the United States of America

In the Summer of 1985 I travelled to northern Poland, in the area of East Prussia, with a group of some thirty Germans. Most of these people had at one time lived in the German provinces east of the Oder-Neisse Line, and as we traveled from town to town many came upon homes from which they, their parents, family and friends had been expelled forty years before. In a tiny hamlet on the road between Allenstein and Marienberg (known presently as Olsztyn and Malbork) our bus stopped in front of a small brick church. An elderly couple hesitantly stepped off of the bus and entered the church, the place of their marriage many years before. As the wife peered around the warm interior of the church, supported on the arm of her husband, she burst into sobs and ran from the building. Not one of us left the churchyard with a dry eye.

The scene in that tiny church in a remote hamlet in Polish-occupied East Prussia will live in this author's memory forever. This work is dedicated to that couple and to the other members of the Rautenberg Reisen group. These men and women gave me more insight into the tragedy of the Oder-Neisse Line than any legal text. It is hoped that this and other written works will assure that never again will people be forced out of their homelands against their will.

CONTENTS

BOUNDARIES IN 1370

BOUNDARIES IN 1750

CHANGES IN BOUNDARIES: 1919 - 1936

THE SITUATION SINCE 1945

1

INTRODUCTION

Territorial disputes on the continent of Europe have always been commonplace, and boundaries are forever changing with the shift in centers of power. Only in recent centuries have scholars begun to question such transfers from a legal perspective, or rather, only in recent times has the legality of territorial transfers made under duress or force been discussed in legal circles. Even so, the majority of territorial changes undertaken in Europe have gone juridically unchallenged, and most are perhaps legally unassailable, due to their validation by treaties or other universally recognized forms of transfer of title. The Treaty of Versailles, signed in 1919 to terminate the greatest conflict known to that date in Europe, made the most controversial territorial changes in Europe ever attempted, and for the first time opened to question the legality of transferring large territories to certain states. However, no disputes arising out of the settlement of World War One would produce such conflicting legal arguments as the most radical boundary change emerging from the Second World War. This boundary dispute is that between Germany and Poland.

We are speaking here of territory in the eastern part of Germany (as that state existed between 1923 and 1937) which since 1945 has been occupied, or some would say annexed, by Poland and the Soviet Union up to a line formed by the rivers Oder and Western (Lausatian) Neisse. The vast area of land between the eastern boundary of Germany in 1937 and the Oder-Neisse Line, some 79,500 square kilometers which contained in 1939 over twelve million inhabitants, comprises the ancient provinces of East Prussia, Pomerania, Silesia and East Brandenburg[1]. Few legal disputes over territorial changes have had such longevity as that over the Oder-Neisse Territories. This is due mainly to the historical development

of their legal status, outlined below. Numerous conferences held between the Allied Powers during the Second World War contained on their agendas discussion of changes in the Polish-German frontier, which all parties expected to be set out in a peace treaty as they had after World War One. At the most important of these conferences, those of Yalta and Potsdam, vague and tentative statements were made as to the new frontier, with the understanding that its final determination would await the peace conference. Unfortunately that peace conference never took place. Due to the East-West split and the Cold War, the former Allied Powers could never come together to draw up a final treaty of peace with Germany. For the same reasons, a united German state and government did not exist with which to conclude a treaty. East and West Germany each emerged as apparant separate nations, neither clearly a successor to the Third Reich. In the meantime Poland and the Soviet Union occupied the Oder-Neisse Territories and proclaimed annexation without a treaty. In the most tragic episode of this dispute, the occupying/annexing states expelled the native German inhabitants of the Territories in a most inhumane fashion.

Sides were then taken. In 1950 East Germany and Poland signed the Gorlitz Treaty that "recognized" the new boundary as set down at Potsdam. West Germany and the Western Powers refused to recognize this change. Between 1945 and 1970 a well-balanced case existed for the legal invalidity of the final territorial settlement, as even the proponents of the settlement recognized the lack of a treaty with a united sovereign Germany and non-recognition by most of the World. However, in 1970 West Germany signed the Treaty of Warsaw with Poland and the Treaty of Moscow with the Soviet Union that by their wording apparantly acceed to the present boundary situation. Since 1971 the legal discussion of the Oder-Neisse Problem has dwindled to a trickle, and today many students of international law and politics may not even have heard of the issue. All of the pro-Polish advocates consider the problem to have been settled once and for all in 1970. Even a number of German advocates find no more fuel for their fire. Has this legal issue really been settled? Were the events in and prior to 1945 enough to produce a valid transfer of territory under international law? At least as important, did the treaties of 1970 end all possible legal challenge to a de facto situation created some twenty-five years before? In sum, is the transfer of the German territories east of the Oder-Neisse Line valid under international law, or is their occupation by Poland and the Soviet Union today, forty-three years after the end of the Second World War, legally invalid and the greatest travesty of justice to ever occur in European territorial disputes?

Notes

1. We shall be dealing here exclusively with the dispute over the territory lost by Germany to Poland and the Soviet Union after World War Two, and not with the Provinces of West Prussia and Posen, given to Poland by the Treaty of Versailles in 1919.

2

HISTORY OF THE ODER-NEISSE TERRITORIES TO 1945

The ethnic composition of Europe has changed drastically over the centuries, no more so than in central and eastern Europe. In the earliest records relating to the area of the Oder-Neisse Territories the configuration of nationalities appears to have been very different than today, or in 1945, and the inhabitants were not of uniform ethnic makeup over the entire breadth of the present territories.

The area of East Prussia was inhabited from ancient times by the Prussians, a Baltic tribe closely related to the Lithuanians. The first written record of this tribe was made by the Roman scholar Tacitus in his *Germania*, written in 69 A.D. In this work he mentions the Aestii, who collected amber along the Baltic and traded with the Roman Empire[1]. The accounts of Tacitus and other ancient travellers are borne out by modern archeological and scientific studies of the ancient Balts. These tribes arrived along the eastern shore of the Baltic Sea before 600 B.C., and the Prussians settled in the territory between the Vistula and Niemen Rivers between 600 and 400 B.C. At this time the area between the Oder River and the Dnieper River was inhabited almost exclusively by Balts. The Slavs were living in what is today the Ukraine, and it was the later westward migration of the Slavs that caused the Balts to be forced westward against the sea[2]. Modern scholarship has established that the Balts were not ethnically related to the Slavs in any manner[3]. There is also ample evidence that the Prussians, known also as Old Prussians (to distinguish them from the later German inhabitants of this area), were of the Baltic family. Enough of their language and civilization remained into the late Middle Ages to show a distinct culture[4]. While some scholars dispute the

fact that the Prussians were a separate nationality like the Lithuanians or Poles[5], no one in recent times has put forward an argument that the Prussians were the ancestors of the present inhabitants of East Prussia, Germans or Poles. Once the Prussians settled in the East Prussian region some time before the First Millenium A.D., they remained in the same territory until the arrival of the crusading Teutonic Knights in the Middle Ages. The Prussian tribe in fact occupied almost precisely the territorial limits that later became the Duchy of Prussia[6], and later still the German province of East Prussia. This boundary is perhaps one of the oldest in Europe, substantially unchanged from ancient times until 1945, even though the inhabitants on both sides of the frontier were replaced over time.

The ethnic origins of Pomerania and Silesia were different than East Prussia in that these territories were not continuously occupied by one nation from ancient times to the German era. Their history is instead wrapped in the controversy over the origins of the Slavs and Germans, and what areas of Europe they inhabited at what time. Both Germans and Slavs migrated from the Eurasian steppes around 2000 B.C., but the Slavs moved westward, pushing the Balts before them, while the Germans went north into Scandinavia[7]. There is no certainty as to how far west the Slavs had migrated at any given period[8]. The Germans, meanwhile, apparently moved into central Europe from Scandinavia and for the first time came into direct contact with the Slavs. While most of central and eastern Europe was inhabited by the Celts until almost the first millenium A.D., there are indications that Germanic tribes began to settle along the Baltic coast of northern Germany during early Roman times[9]. In the "race" between Teuton and Slav as to who was the first to inhabit the area of the Oder-Neisse Territories, the winner may be difficult to determine. However, the most recent scholarship on the Slavic migrations seems to indicate that when the Slavs entered central Europe, they bumped up against the Germans who were already there and had long been trading with the Roman Empire. East Teutonic tribes, including the Vandals, Burgundians and Rugii, inhabited all of what is present-day Poland during the Second and First Centuries B.C. They were in turn replaced by the Germanic Goths, who migrated from Scandinavia in the First Century A.D, and did not leave the area until the Third Century[10]. Thus the Slavs may have settled in present-day Poland by expelling the prior inhabitants, most likely Germans[11].

By 1100 A.D. there was little territory east of the Elbe River inhabited by Germans. The nature of the inhabitants outside of East Prussia is open to question. Many historians argue that Slavs, such as Wends and Poles, occupied land from the Dnieper to the Elbe[12]. On the other hand, Tacitus

describes the inhabitants of Pomerania, the Suevi, as closely resembling the Aestii, or Prussians[13], and in fact Pomerania existed as an independent kingdom until its occupation by Prussia in the Middle Ages, never forming a part of the first organised Polish state (although Pomerania was a Polish fief between 1000 and 1200). Recent studies have clarified that the region of Silesia was inhabited during this period by the Sorbs and Chrobidites, and the Abrodites or their descendants inhabited Pomerania. The Polish Slavs were confined to areas south and east of the Vistula.

The historic event most often recounted by Germanophobes and proponents of Polish claims to eastern Germany is the *Drang Nach Osten*. About 1000 A.D. German settlers, supported by various German princes, began to migrate into lands east of the Elbe River that were inhabited by the Slavic Wends. This settlement program, suffering some setbacks and accompanied by missionaries and warriors, caused all of what is today East Germany to be dominated by Germans under the Holy Roman Empire by about 1200. More importantly, a substantial portion of Pomerania and Silesia became predominantly German[14]. In the case of these two provinces, many German settlers were invited to settle in the area by the ruling Slavic princes. Some of these territories were sparsely inhabited, and the local rulers were in need of skilled German farmers and craftsmen to strengthen their hold on the area. Silesia at this time was part of the Kingdom of Bohemia, a member of the Holy Roman Empire that had conquered the Province between 929 and 967 A.D.[15]. In 1526 the Kingdom of Bohemia, which included all of Silesia, was absorbed into the Habsburg Empire[16]. Silesia was in turn taken from Austria by Prussia during the reign of Frederick the Great after a lengthy war which ended in 1742 [17]. Pomerania maintained its status as an independent duchy until it was absorbed by Prussia in the Fifteenth Century, having been a part of the Holy Roman Empire before 1200 [18]. The first unified Polish kingdom emerged around 1000, and at no time included Pomerania or Silesia, as these were absorbed into the Holy Roman Empire, of which Poland was never a part.

Brandenburg was the first portion of the Oder-Neisse Territories to become part of a German state. The March of Brandenburg, as it was known before the Holy Roman Emperor made it an electorate, was created in the era of Charlamagne and straddled the Oder River, including territory from the Elbe in the west to the middle of eastern Pomerania and the future western border of Poznan in the east, separating Pomerania and Silesia[19].

The transition of East Prussia into a German province was much clearer. In 1229 the Polish Duke of Mazovia[20], having continuously fought against incursions from Prussian raiders, invited the Teutonic Order, a

German military-monastic order that had formed for the crusades in the Levant, to conquor and Christianize Prussia. In return the Order was given title to the Kulmerland, in south-west East Prussia, any further territory in Prussia that it subjugated, and the Duke's blessing to rule as it saw fit[21]. Between 1230 and 1422 the Teutonic Knights conquered and subjugated the Prussians, and swarms of German settlers were introduced into the land. By war, extermination and intermarriage Germans almost completely replaced the ancient Prussians by 1525, when the Order was dissolved and Prussia became a secular duchy[22]. The last pure Prussians probably died out around 1700 [23].

The Teutonic Order continuously fought with the rising powers of Poland and Lithuania. During the Fourteenth Century the Teutonic Order expanded outward from the narrow confines of East Prussia to control lands as far west as the pre-1939 eastern border of Pomerania, in effect the entire territory of the future province of West Prussia, known to the Poles as Royal Prussia, including the important commercial city of Danzig. During this period the Hanseatic League took over the port cities of Danzig, Elbing, Königsberg and Memel, so that their populations boomed and became almost exclusively German. All of these cities except Elbing had been founded by the Teutonic Order, and were for all practical purposes as German as Hamburg or Bremen.

When the Treaty of Thorn was signed in 1466, fifty-six years after the Order's military defeat by the Poles and Lithuanians at the Battle of Tannenburg, the Order lands were reduced to the area of the later province of East Prussia, minus the territories of Ermland and Marienburg (which had been the areas of earliest occupation by the Order in Prussia), and Prussia became a fief of Poland. There is every indication that the population continued to be predominantly German or German-Prussian. The rest of the frontier, however, from Kulm around to Memel, remained unchanged from 1310, or in fact from ancient times when there was no true frontier, but rather an ethnic separation between Prussians and Lithuanians[24]. Also, Prussia retained direct German rule, and the population became increasingly German[25]. In 1620 Prussia, by then ruled by the same Hohenzollern dynasty that ruled Brandenburg, was absorbed into the Kingdom of Prussia, although it always remained outside of the Holy Roman Empire[26].

Most historians and international legal theorists consider that the Treaty of Westphalia in 1648 marked the beginning of the modern nation-state. Therefore, only after this date can we be sure that modern legal theory will apply to the problem of territorial relations between political entities. By this time the frontiers of the Oder-Neisse Territories had long been established, but the eastern frontier of Germany would once more

move eastward against Poland. In 1772 Prussia, Austria and Russia, citing concern over the safety of national minorities within the chaotic and disintegrating Polish Kingdom, occupied by prearrangement among themselves certain areas of Poland and enacted the First Partition of Poland (this would not be the last time such a pretext for intervention would be used in this region of Europe). Prussia's share included the territory of West Prussia minus the city of Danzig, which had been lost in the Treaty of Thorn. The Ermland was thus restored to East Prussia. In 1793 and 1795 the three powers conducted the Second and Third Partitions of Poland, completely eliminating the Kingdom of Poland from the map of Europe. In the Second Partition Prussia received the province of Posen plus the city of Danzig, and in the Third Partition Prussia received a territory southeast of East Prussia known as New East Prussia[27]. Most of the land obtained by Prussia in the Partitions had never before been occupied by a German state. The exceptions were the area taken in the First Partition, which was merely a recovery from the Peace of Thorn, and the city of Danzig taken in the Second Partition. The territory of New East Prussia was returned to Poland (the short-lived Republic of Warsaw) by Napoleon in 1805 after his defeat of Prussia, and was never recovered by Prussia. Posen was also returned to Poland in 1805, but in 1815 at the Congress of Vienna it was once more handed to Prussia, which would retain Posen until 1919. Significantly, even Napoleon did not consider returning West Prussia or other territories to Poland, although it too was handed to Poland in 1919 to form the infamous "Polish Corridor", separating East Prussia from the rest of Germany. The only territories obtained by Prussia in the Polish Partitions that would form part of the future Oder-Neisse Territories were the Ermland, Marienburg and the city of Danzig, all at one time part of the lands of the Teutonic Order, and all retained by Prussia (or Germany) uninterrupted between 1772 and 1945. Thus, even if the Partitions of Poland are found to have been illegal by modern principles of international law (and this is a strong possibility), their significance to the question of the Oder-Neisse Territories is minimal at best.

When Prussia was unified with the rest of Germany by Chancellor Bismarck in 1871 the Oder-Neisse Territories became part of the German Empire[28]. In 1919 Germany signed the Treaty of Versailles ending World War One. This Treaty stipulated that the provinces of Posen and West Prussia would be given to the newly-reconstituted Poland, and that Danzig would become a free city with special Polish prerogatives. Most significantly, however, the Treaty of Versailles called for plebiscites to be held in Upper Silesia, Marienwerder and southern East Prussia (the so-called Allenstein region), in which the population of these regions would

vote to remain German or become part of Poland. Each area was a part of the Oder-Neisse Territories that bordered the new Poland and contained significant Polish populations. The plebiscites were held under strict League of Nations supervision, with French and British troops in occupation to maintain order. Needless to say there was little sympathy among the League members for the German cause, and in fact Polish propaganda was readily allowed, while German campaigning was strictly curtailed[29]. Nonetheless, the results of the plebiscites were to most observers astounding. The plebiscites in Marienwerder and Allenstein (southern East Prussia) were held on July 11, 1920. In Marienwerder 96,923 votes were cast in favor of Germany, and 8,018 in favor of Poland, which meant that 92.4% of the voters favored Germany[30]. Allenstein province showed even greater support for Germany. There 363,209 votes fell for Germany and 7,980 went for Poland, giving Germany 97.9% of the vote[31]!

The plebiscite in Upper Silesia was not so easily handled. Here there was a much more distinct Polish minority due to the large number of mines and factories that attracted cheap Polish labor. In some border towns of Upper Silesia Poles made up almost 100% of the population[32]. The time between the end of the First World War and the Silesian plebiscite held on March 20, 1921 was marked by intense violence by both Poles and Germans and every type of fraud, coercion and intimidation imaginable. The League forces stationed there had their hands full controlling the situation. German attempts at propaganda were usually more severely dealt with than Polish actions, which led to charges of League bias. When the vote was finally taken, 707,605 votes, or 59.6%, went to Germany and 479,359, or 40.3%, went to Poland[33]. While the plebiscite indicated a majority for Germany, the League Commission was not satisfied that the results should allow Germany to retain the entire area, and so a compromise was worked out whereby Upper Silesia was partitioned between Germany and Poland. Poland received the supposedly pro-Polish districts, although each state thereby retained a substantial minority of the other's nationality, as the ethnic division in Upper Silesia was between cities and small towns, rather than along clear district lines[34].

One other area was severed from the Oder-Neisse Territories in 1919, namely the Memel Territory, a strip of land in northern East Prussia bordering on Lithuania. The Treaty of Versailles envisioned that this land would become a free state like Danzig. It was maintained by the League of Nations until 1924, when the Lithuanian army occupied it and Lithuania unilaterally annexed the region without League consent, but with no protest. That same year Lithuania and the League signed the Klaipeda Convention, which made the Memel (or Klaipeda) Territory a

protectorate of Lithuania, stipulating that the territory would be autonomous, not annexed outright[35]. Subsequent Lithuanian rule in the Territory gave no indication of this special status, even though Memel's autonomy was legally confirmed by the Permanent Court of International Justice in 1932 [36]. A 1920 census indicated that there were 71,156 Germans, 67,259 Lithuanians and 126 Poles living in the region at that time[37]. In 1938 Lithuania signed the Treaty Between the Republic of Lithuania and the Reich of Germany Concerning the Transfer of the Territory of Klaipeda whereby she returned the Memelland to Germany[38]. The Memelland thereby became the only part of the German eastern territories lost after World War One that was returned to Germany peacefully.

Few historians will argue that the recovery of the lands lost to Poland after World War One was the primary reason that Germany invaded Poland in 1939. There is little point in recounting the many atrocities committed by the Germans during their five-year occupation of Poland, nor the German-Russian intention of conducting the fourth partition of Poland in 1939. The victory of the Allied and Associated Powers in 1945 assured that Germany would not retain her wartime conquests. However, even prior to Germany's surrender, indeed only shortly after the beginning of World War Two, many statesmen from Poland and elsewhere began to speak of a further change in the pre-1939 borders in favor of Poland. It is the intention of this author that the *legal* basis for the post-1945 frontiers be analyzed in depth. Many advocates on both sides of the dispute put forward elaborate moral, historical, geographic and ethical reasons to justify their positions. In any analysis of this complex problem we can not avoid addressing some of the more firmly grounded non-legal arguments, as they may bear directly on the legal problem. No issue of this magnitude, with the number of persons involved or with such deep roots, can be thoroughly dealt with on stark legal grounds alone. It is hoped that the academic necessity of these other arguments will also be recognized[39].

Notes

1. Alfred Church, ed. *The Agricola and Germany of Tacitus*, 119 (1911).

2. Glyn Daniel, *The Balts*, 83 (1963).

3. Archeological studies of their culture give ample evidence of their difference since earliest times. See for example Marija Gimbutas, *The Balts* (1963) and Albertas Gerutas, *Lithuania: 700 Years*, 1-33 (1984). Gerutas relies upon linguistic studies as well as archeology.

4. William Schmalstieg, *Studies in Old Prussian* (1976). This study is also based as much on linguistics as anthropology.

5. Constantine Jurgela, in his *History of the Lithuanian Nation*, 18 (1948), argues that "it is a historic fallacy to attribute a distinct nationality or language to the 'Old Prussians'", and states that they were identical with the Lithuanians. This is probably the most substantial attack on the idea that the area of East Prussia was inhabited by an independent nationality, and yet no claim is made for an ancient Slav culture in this region. In fact, no serious argument has ever been made for an ethnic Slavic, much less Polish, connection with East Prussia.

6. "Prussians", *Encyclopedia Lituanica* 366-68.

7. Frank Kmietowicz, *Ancient Slavs*, 11 (1976).

8. There is some indication of at least proto-Slavic cultures in the region between the upper Elbe and the Vistula, known as the Lusatian culture, between 600 and 400 B.C. See: Kmietowicz, *supra* at 47-50. On the other hand, the renouned classical historian Michael Grant maintains that even as late as 500 A.D. the Slavs' westernmost reach corresponded roughly to the pre-1939 western frontiers of Poland and Russia. See: Michael Grant, *Ancient History Atlas*, 86-87 (1981). Most historians agree that the "Slavs" that migrated westward were a disunited collection of tribes and petty-kingdoms that formed no central nation. Thus the actual location of the ancestors of the modern Polish state will never be precisely known prior to the early Middle Ages.

9. Herbert Schutz, *The Prehistory of Germanic Europe*, 153-56 (1983), places this settlement at around 450 B.C. German historians, such as Fritz Gause, *Geschichte des Preussenlandes*, 8-12 (1966), place Germanic tribes as far east as the Vistula and south to the Carpathians between 800 and 300 B.C, while still admitting to the mysterious Lausitzer culture bordering on them to the south and east, and the Balts in East Prussia.

10. Jan Czarnecki, *The Goths in Ancient Poland* (1975).

11. Francis Dvornik, *The Slavs in European History and Civilization*, 1-4 (1962). Here it is argued that the Germanic tribes were on the European scene several centuries before the Slavs. In W.F. Reddaway, et. al. (ed.), *The Cambridge History of Poland*, 2 (1950), even Russian academics are cited for the premise that when the Slavs first moved into Poland they took over territory vacated, voluntarily or otherwise, by Goths and other Germanic tribes.

12. Joachim Herrmann, "The Northern Slavs", David Wilson (ed.) *The Northern World*, 194-95 (1980); Norman Pounds, *Eastern Europe*, 44-45 (1969).

13. Church, *Supra*, P.120.

14. James Thompson, "East German Colonization in the Middle Ages", *Annual Report of the American Historical Association, 1915*, 125-150 (1916). Thompson gives a good summary of the entire movement from the end of Charlemagne's reign to the time of the Teutonic Knights in Prussia. The numerous instances of German trickery in obtaining land from the Slavs, the confusing or broken treaties, and wars and revolts are recounted. What is noteworthy in Thompson's article is that he likens the German eastward colonization to the westward expansion of the United States against the American Indians in the Nineteenth Century, and, even more relevant to the time of the writing, to the European colonization of Africa and Asia. While Thompson does not discuss the origins of the different nationalities, he clearly believes that the towns of eastern Germany, and the land, was firmly Slav at the time of the movement, and that all land east of the Elbe had to be Germanized later.

15. John Bradley, *Czechoslavakia*, 11 (1971). Apparantly even at this early stage a significant portion of the population was German, as was the population of Bohemia proper. For the Polish argument that Silesia remained ethnically Polish for a longer period, and that the province was not completely absorbed into the Bohemian Kingdom until the Fourteenth Century, see various articles in: Karola Maleczynskiego, *Historia Slaska* (1961).

16. *Id.* at 67. The Czech Diet elected the Habsburg ruler of Austria to the throne of Bohemia to obtain a powerful ruling house that would protect Bohemia from her neighbors.

17. H. W. Koch, *A History of Prussia*, 114 (1978).
Lower and Upper Silesia were ceded to Prussia by Austria under the preliminary Peace of Breslau, signed in June, 1742, and confirmed by the "permanent" Peace of Berlin in July, 1742. Robert Kann, *A History of the Habsburg Empire*, 98 (1977). This appears to be the first instance where a preliminary agreement was reached on a territorial question, to be followed by the confirmation of the annexation later. Apparantly Austria considered the territorial losses of the Peace of Breslau to be temporary, and only with the Peace of Berlin did she actually relinquish claims to Silesia (although Austria would later try to reconquor Silesia in the Seven Year's War). Neither side considered the transfer final until the Berlin agreement.

18. Francis Carsten, *The Origins of Prussia*, 2 (1981).

19. Koch, *supra* at 23.

20. A territory bordering East Prussia to the south.

21. This would seem mere verbiage, for the Duke of Mazovia never held sway over the Prussians, and thus could not actually give away territory.

22. For details of the Germanization of Prussia under the Teutonic Order, see: Christian Krollmann, *The Teutonic Order in Prussia*, (1938); Sidney Fay, *The Rise of Brandenburg-Prussia to 1786*, (1937); Herbert Tuttle, *History of Prussia*, (1884). For the extreme German nationalist view of the Teutonic Order in Prussia, see: Treitske, *The Origins of Prussianism* (1905).

23. "Prussians", *Encyclopedia Lituanica*, 371.

24. Jonas A. Stiklorius, "Lithuania Minor in International Treaties", *Lithuania Minor*, 11-29 (1976).

25. By 1500 most of northern and western East Prussia, as well as about one half of Pomerania and all of Silesia except for the easternmost tip, were predominantly or exclusively German-inhabited. Norman Pounds, *Eastern Europe*, 49 (1969).

26. Legal sources are devoid of detailed analyses of the legal status of a "fief" in medieval times. Under the fiefdom set up by the Treaty of Thorn, the Teutonic Order retained absolute control over Prussia, and in fact engaged in some minor wars with Lithuania. After the Teutonic Order was dissolved in 1525 with the coming of the Reformation, Prussia became a duchy and was ruled by hereditary houses. Eventually the dukedom fell by inheritance to the Hohenzollerns of Brandenburg. While historical maps indicate that West Prussia and the Ermland were incorporated into Poland proper, Prussia always retained an independent status. This situation is not unrealistic, considering that while the Order may have lost several battles with the Poles, the Poles were never able to occupy a significant portion of Prussia, nor to totally defeat the Order's armies.

27. For a full description of the three partitions see: Norman Davies, *God's Playground: A History of Poland*, Vol. I, 511-546 (1982); Lord Eversley, *The Partitions of Poland*, (1973) and Oscar Halecki, *Borderlands of Western Civilization*, 258-275 (1952).

28. Under the Empire the Polish regions of Germany were subjected to harsh Germanization efforts, spurred on at first by the ultra-nationalistic H-K-T Society, which demanded abolition of the use of the Polish language in government and schools and, later, expropriation of many Polish land holdings. The anti-Catholic Bismarckian "Kulturkampf" added fuel to the fire of anti-Polish feeling. Most of this activity was confined to Posen and West Prussia, which were still heavily populated by Poles, and thus this conflict had little direct impact on the Oder-Neisse Territories (except in the Polish regions of Upper Silesia and East Prussia, the last areas of significant Polish settlement in the Oder-Neisse Territories). Nevertheless the damage that this policy did to Polish-German relations would return to haunt the hapless German civilians in the Oder-Neisse Territories in 1945 when the Poles set up their anti-German administration. See: Richard Wonser Tims, *Germanizing Prussian Poland*, (1966). For a detailed analysis of the ethnic makeup of Posen and West Prussia just before the First World War, which shows the significant Polish majority in those territories, see: Manfred Laubert, *Nationalitat und Volkswille im Preussischen Osten*, (1925). For the understandably negative Polish view of German policies in the eastern provinces, see: Waclaw Sobanski, *Western and Northern Territories of Poland, Demographic Problems, Part I*, 8-22 (1959).This latter work also gives an interesting argument showing a supposed shortage of manpower in the German provinces due to a flight of the German population from the east *before* the Second World War, and a terribly bad overpopulation problem in Polish provinces bordering the German territory. This is used to justify the post-1945 transfer of the remaining German population to benefit the "more needy" Polish population.

29. Sarah Wambaugh, *Plebiscites Since the World War* (two vol.), Vol. 1 (1933).

30. Wambaugh, *Supra*, P.133; Gause, *Supra*, P.85.

31. *Id*.

32. This statement is made based upon the actual plebiscite results in individual towns. See: Wambaugh, supra at 258. Most of the Polish majority lived in rural areas along the frontier, and most towns and "Kreise" in the middle of Upper Silesia were majority German.

33. Wambaugh, *Supra*, P.250. About 3,882 ballots were declared void.

34. Wambaugh, supra at 263-270. For a discussion of the plebiscite idea in the post-war peace treaties, see: Johannes Mattern, "The Employment of the Plebiscite in the Determination of Sovereignty", *Johns Hopkins University Studies in Historical and Political Science, Vol. XXXVIII*, 128-150 (1920).

35. Stiklorius, *Supra*, P.47-50.

36. *Interpretation of the Statute of the Memel Territory*. P.C.I.J. Ser. A./B, No.49 (1932).

37. Johann von Leers, *Memelland*, P.7 (1932).

38. *Id*.

39. For a review of the wartime opinions of various spokesmen for the Polish, Soviet and Western governments, see: P. Buhler, "The Rape of Central Europe: The Oder-Neisse Line and the Amputation of Eastern Germany, 1941-1950",

(1983) (available in College of William and Mary Dept. of Government Library, and from the author). One of the best short summaries of the history of the Oder-Neisse Territories, from the earliest times to the post-World War Two period, as well as economic, geographic and population statistics, can be found in: Rep. Reece, "On German Provinces East of the Oder-Neisse Line, and Economic, Historical, Legal and Political Aspects Involved", 103 *Congressional Record* 7117 (1957).

3

THE LEGAL STATUS OF THE ODER-NEISSE TERRITORIES PRIOR TO THE WARSAW AND MOSCOW TREATIES (1945-1970)

The idea of giving part of the German provinces of Silesia, Pomerania and East Prussia to Poland was not a child of the post-1945 period. As early as 1919, when the Treaty of Versailles established the new Poland, some authorities, albeit Polish nationalists, were calling for a frontier with Germany further west than that actually established[1], and some advocated a return to the Carolingian frontier on the Elbe! It is not surprising that scarcely two months after the outbreak of World War Two with the German invasion of Poland the Polish government began to call for a rectification of the border in Poland's favor, which indicated an intention to move westward at Germany's expense[2]. This position was taken up by Poles everywhere, including the exile press[3]. Nevertheless, in the first wartime meeting between Churchill and Roosevelt as heads of the Western Alliance, the two nations drafted the Atlantic Charter, a document that would set new goals for postwar relations between states. This agreement in pertinent part states: "First, their countries seek no aggrandizement, territorial or other; second, they desire to see no territorial changes that do not accord with the freely expressed wishes of the peoples concerned."[4]. Both the Soviet Union and Poland later became parties to the Atlantic Charter, and in 1942 they both signed the United Nations Declaration, which embodied the principles of the Atlantic Charter. German protagonists have since used this document to attempt to show that the Allies intended, in fact legally agreed, that no territorial

changes would be implemented at the expense of Germany[5], and more importantly that such territorial changes would not be undertaken unless and until the population concerned agreed. In fact this concept was not entirely new. Towards the end of World War One President Wilson had proposed a similar guarantee of self-determination to populations in territorial matters in his Fourteen Points. The difference is that the Fourteen Points was not, as an international agreement, ever adopted in full by the Allied Powers, although parts were included in the Treaty of Versailles. The interesting aspect of the Fourteen Points is that Wilson made specific exceptions to the principle of self-determination when territorial changes for strategic or other reasons were necessary. He specifically called for a "free and independent Poland" with guaranteed access to the sea, which in 1918 would require the annexation of certain German lands along the Baltic that contained German majorities[6]. The only other annexation imposed by Versailles without a plebiscite or other recognition of ethnic interests was the return of Alsace-Lorraine to France, which had already been specifically mentioned in the Fourteen Points[7]. On the other hand, the Atlantic Charter makes no specific exceptions for territorial changes that do not accord with the "freely expressed wishes" of the populations concerned, as was done with West Prussia and Alsace-Lorraine in 1919.

Polish protagonists maintain that the Atlantic Charter was never meant to apply to Germany, and thus any territorial changes at Germany's expense would be considered automatic exceptions to the principles of the Atlantic Charter. The strongest support for this claim comes from the statements of Prime Minister Churchill in the House of Commons later in the War. On February 22, 1944 he announced that "(t)here will be...no question of the Atlantic Charter applying to Germany as a matter of right and barring territorial transferences or adjustments in enemy countries."[8]. This position was supported soon afterward by British Foreign Secretary Eden who commented:

> ...Germany would not, as a matter of right, be able to claim to benefit from the Atlantic Charter in such a way as to preclude the victorious Powers from making territorial adjustments at her expense...we can not admit that Germany can claim, as a matter of right on her part...that any part of the Charter applies to her.[9]

Leading Polish scholars believe that these retrospective statements conclusively prove that the Atlantic Charter was never meant to apply to Germany[10]. The question to be asked is whether post-enactment statements are authoritative in interpreting the meaning of an

international agreement when they conflict with established state practice. It must be conceeded that the concept of national "self-determination" is primarily a Twentieth Century phenomena, and thus its status as established state practice is open to question. Evidence of its place among the law of nations comes mostly from the Treaty of Versailles. In our case, if the signatories to the Atlantic Charter had intended that it not apply to Germany, why did they not indicate their intention in the document? In fact, some of the subsequent signatories to the Charter announced specific reservations, which are used as further support by the Polish and Russian protagonists. When Poland and Czechoslovakia signed the Charter they issued a joint declaration hoping that the Charter would be applied "in the spirit of justice which does not admit the uniformity of treatment of those guilty of provoking world wars and of the victims of these wars"[11]. The Soviet Union made a more vague reservation in stating that "these principles will necessarily adapt itself (sic) to the circumstances, needs, and historic peculiarities of particular countries"[12]. Even if the reservations made at the time the Charter was signed are valid, all of the signatories are bound by substantially the same provisions as they were later embodied in the Charter of the United Nations. Both the prohibition of the forceful transfer of territory (Article 2(4)) and the support for self-determination of peoples (Article 55) are part of the United Nations Charter[13]. Unlike the Atlantic Charter, no signatories submitted (or were allowed to submit) reservations to the U.N. Charter[14]. The U.N. Charter was built from the framework of the Dumbarton Oaks Conference in late 1944, in which the Soviet Union participated and agreed in principle. The resolutions of this conference were published before the Yalta and Potsdam Conferences, which were the most important Allied conferences relating to the Oder-Neisse Line. The U.N. Charter was signed and entered into force in San Francisco on June 26, 1945, and had at that point been adhered to by Poland and the Soviet Union[15]. This Charter was thus effective and binding upon its members prior to the conclusion of the Potsdam Conference, which the Polish protagonists usually hold to be the Conference that legally created the Oder-Neisse frontier. If Germany was meant to be excluded from the benefits and protection of the U.N. Charter principles, in similar fashion to the Atlantic Charter, then this document will have no bearing on the legality of the Polish-German frontier[16]. On the other hand, if the Charter of the U.N. is recognized as codifying the proper norms of international law as recognised by modern states, then even a state that has itself violated those principles may not be excluded from the protection of international law. The spirit of the U.N. could not condone the correction of one wrong by committing another. Ancient Roman law recognized the principle "Ex injuria non oritur jus",

or "no right can come out of a wrong". Thus an annexation by force of arms is a wrong under international law, and legal title to such territory will never become valid. If Germany is made to be one exception to the principles adopted at San Francisco, this would give precedent for other "exceptions". Even if the U.N. Charter does not codify existing international law but instead creates a new code of conduct, it would still be relevant to this dispute, as the Charter was signed only one month and one week before the Potsdam Declaration was issued, and only one week before the opening of the Potsdam Conference that allegedly decided the fate of the Oder-Neisse Territories. The law of the U.N. Charter was thus in force for the Potsdam delegates. If either the Atlantic Charter or the U.N. Charter were to be found to apply to Germany in 1945, all of the conference decisions that will be reviewed below would be found invalid as conflicting with recognised international law. Furthermore, if either Charter was a codification of accepted norms of international law at the time, and they certainly became the guiding principles after 1945, then the annexations allegedly sanctioned by subsequent agreements, in violation of the principles of self-determination of peoples and peaceful resolution of disputes, would be a nullity. This proposition was recognized by most of the signatories to the U.N. Charter in the Vienna Convention on the Law of Treaties, signed in 1969 and considered by most to be a codification of existing law, not a new set of principles[17].

Conquest in principle has been viewed by many states as a prohibited practice since at least 1945. Apart from its prohibition by the U.N. Charter and various regional conventions signed before World War Two, there is no better example of the invalidity of acquiring territory by conquest then the nullification of the annexations made by the Axis Powers during World War Two. Although considerable territories were acquired by Hungary, Bulgaria and Germany, some made legal by the Vienna Awards of 1940 which was signed by the states acquiring and ceding the territories, the Allies had no trouble declaring all of these changes void in 1945. Even earlier the Treaty of Versailles voided the German annexation of territory from Russia pursuant to the Treaty of Brest-Litovsk of 1918[18]. It is hardly arguable that Poland and the Soviet Union "conquered" eastern Germany in 1945, and while the Soviet Union took up an occupation zone in accord with Allied agreements reached earlier (see below), Poland's occupation was one of pure conquest and military presence. Dr. Whiteman notes that in such a situation "the territory thus conquered is regarded as in a state of military occupation, and the legal transfer of sovereignty must await the formal annexation by the conquering state."[19]. The Poles claim that this formal annexation took place as a result of the Potsdam and other wartime Conferences. Whether such conferences vested legal title with the

conquerors remains one of the most hotly debated issues in the Oder-Neisse controversy.

The first Allied wartime conference to address postwar boundary questions was the Teheran Conference, held between November 28 and December 1, 1943. Prior to this conference discussion between the Big Three with regard to the Polish-German frontier had been limited to possible separation of East Prussia, Danzig and Upper Silesia from Germany[20]. On the first day of the session, however, Stalin proposed that the Polish frontier could be moved as far west as the Oder River, which surprised the British and Americans[21]. However, the Western Allies were anxious for a cooperative atmosphere with the Russians, for they feared that otherwise they would have no influence over areas liberated by the Russian army. Relations between the Soviet Union and the London Poles were strained (see below), and if Stalin refused to recognize the London Poles, who were under British influence, the post-war Polish government would be made up of only "Moscow" Poles[22]. Roosevelt did not participate in the detailed discussions of the Polish frontiers, leaving this to Churchill, but apparently the maximum amount of territory that the Americans were willing to give to Poland included East Prussia, Danzig and the Oppeln District of Silesia[23]. Churchill, however, indicated an interest in the Oder River Line. During the Conference he produced a formula stating:

> It is thought in principle that the home of the Polish state and nation should be between the so-called Curzon Line and the Line of the Oder, including for Poland East Prussia and Oppeln; but the actual tracing of the frontier line requires careful study, and possible disentanglement of population at some points.[24]

The Russians brought up the demand for the city of Königsberg and surrounding area for the first time, claiming their need for an ice-free port[25]. The Western Allies did not make any commitment to this, but tried to hinge their acceptance on Russian acceptance of a favorable Polish-Soviet border (see below)[26]. Stalin did not seem enthusiastic about the Oder Line, as he apparently wanted a large Poland only if a government of his choosing was in power[27]. The issue of the expulsion of the German population from annexed territory was also brought up for the first time (this issue will be dealt with in detail in the last chapter).

The declaration issued at the conclusion of the Teheran Conference made no mention of any territorial agreements, specific or general, formalising the obvious lack of agreement among the Big Three[28].

However, several crucial issues emerged during the many hours of the conference in which the Polish-German frontier was actually discussed. First was the new idea of extending the frontier to the Oder River, an idea that Churchill had refused to consider in talks in March, 1943 but now seemed to endorse. Stalin was also able with little trouble to get some consensus on the Russian annexation of Königsberg, although the Russians had no historic or ethnic claim to the area[29].

Perhaps the most important issue to impact on the future of the Oder-Neisse Territories was the Polish-Russian frontier. In 1939 the Soviet Union had joined Germany in the invasion of Poland, pursuant to their secret agreement entered into shortly before. Under the Nazi-Soviet Pact Poland was divided between the two powers, with the Soviet Union obtaining most of Poland east of the Curzon Line (the eastern frontier of Poland proposed at Versailles in 1919, before the Russo-Polish War of 1920-21 that pushed Poland's frontier far to the east)[30]. Much of eastern Poland was inhabited by Byelorussians and Ukrainians, which gave Russia a reason to occupy the territory in 1939 and to claim it later. After Germany invaded Russia in 1941 the Russians recognized the Polish government-in-exile, known as the London Poles, and the question of the post-war frontier between Poland and Russia was temporarily dropped. However, by the time of Teheran relations between the Soviet government and the London Poles were strained[31]. The Russian government became bolder after the formation in 1943 of a rump Polish government in Moscow, made up of Polish Communists who had fled from German-occupied Poland in 1939-40, and other Poles enlisted from those captured by the Russian Army in 1939. This group would become the puppet Lublin Government installed as Soviet forces began to enter Poland in 1944. Overhanging London-Soviet relations was the threat that the Soviet Union would cut off support for the non-Communist London Poles in favor of its own Polish exiles. Thus when Stalin pushed for the Curzon Line as the new Soviet-Polish frontier at Teheran, Churchill and Roosevelt had little objection[32]. They feared that a refusal to grant this concession would completely rupture Soviet-London Polish relations and thus leave the London Poles completely out of post-war Poland[33]. The Western Powers agreed to support the Russian claim to the Curzon Line, even though the Poles were not in attendance at Teheran and were not even consulted[34].

From this grant of a great amount of eastern Polish territory to Russia came the concept of "compensation". In return for the Poles giving up territory east of the Curzon Line, the Soviet Union and the other great powers agreed to support Polish claims for land at the expense of Germany. In effect the state of Poland was pushed westward. How far west was not absolutely clear. As we have seen, Churchill was willing to

give Poland East Prussia and the Oppeln district of Silesia (the area of Upper Silesia retained by Germany after the plebiscite of 1921)[35]. Shortly after the Conference Churchill told Mikolajczyk that he would support Polish claims to the Oder line if the Poles would accept the Curzon Line[36]. Roosevelt apparantly was willing to go along with whatever agreement was reached between the British, Russians and Poles[37]. By the end of the Conference, according to many authorities, the Big Three had agreed in principle to support a Russian-Polish frontier at the Curzon Line and the Polish frontier "up to the Oder River"[38]. This decision, which was formalised at the Yalta and Potsdam Conferences (see below) was the cause of the radical idea of a Polish-German frontier on the Oder River. Even Polish authorities admit:

> It is evident that so great a shift of the western border would not have been possible without the claims that the U.S.S.R. made against almost half the territory of Poland (the ally in whose defense the Western Powers went to war), the subsequent terrible ordeal of the Polish nationals during World War II, and the total destruction of the Polish economy by the Nazis.[39]

The "compensation theory" has no basis in prior state practice, except possibly in friendly treaties where all of the parties involved negotiated and agreed to the settlement for mutual benefit. The westward movement of Poland was decided upon without the participation of either Poland or Germany, the two nations that would lose territory[40]. As a legal argument it is almost devoid of weight.

It must be emphasized that the Teheran Conference was in no way a legally binding agreement, but only an indication of general attitudes that could be used to interpret the later Potsdam decisions. Nevertheless, even here we must question the legality of the Curzon Line in light of the Atlantic Charter. While Germany may have been excepted from application of the Charter provisions, there is no ground to support a similar action with respect to Polish territory, unless the Atlantic Charter is to have no meaning at all. The only plausible argument would be the ethnic makeup of eastern Poland and the right of self-determination that would unite Ukrainians and Byelorussians. Interestingly, no justifications for the annexation were voiced at Teheran.

The first systematic outline of the post-war German-Polish frontier took place at the Yalta Conference between the Big Three, held in February, 1945. Just prior to this conference, however, the British and U.S. foreign ministers met at the Malta Conference to coordinate policies. There British Foreign Secretary Eden and the American delegate Matthews agreed that Poland should receive East Prussia, part of Upper

Silesia, "certain other territories up to the Oder" and "the eastern tip of Pomerania"[41]. Here the Western position on the Oder Line was clarified. Apparantly the Western Powers did not view the Oder Line as including all territory to the east of the River down to Stettin, as all of eastern Pomerania lies east of the Oder. Thus the Western conception of a Polish frontier on the Oder meant a much smaller cession of territory by Germany than envisioned by the Soviets. Also notable was the lack of agreement as to the Western or Lausatian Neisse, or for that matter to either Neisse river[42].

When the Yalta Conference opened Soviet Foreign Minister Molotov outlined the Soviet position on Poland's frontiers:

> 1. ...that the Curzon Line should be the eastern frontier of Poland, with adjustments in some regions of five to eight kilometers in favour of Poland.
> 2. ...that the western frontier of Poland should be drawn from the town of Stettin (which would be Polish), and thence southwards along the river Oder and the Western Neisse.[43]

This proposal did not go over well with Churchill or Roosevelt. It must be remembered also that by this time the Soviets had formally broken ties with the London Poles, and had already set up their own Polish government at Lublin, in liberated eastern Poland. Thus there was little hope for much western influence in post-war Poland, and many writers speculate that this realisation made Churchill, and possibly Roosevelt, resist the grant of any extra territory to what they feared would become a Soviet puppet state[44]. Whether this theory is realistic or not, the British and American positions differed greatly from the Soviet proposal. Contrary to some claims that the Oder-Neisse Line had been agreed upon in principle at Teheran, there were great disputes at Yalta. The Americans favored the Curzon Line plus Lwow in the east, and held that the transfer of German territory in the west should be limited to East Prussia (with Königsberg going to the Soviet Union), Upper Silesia and "a small coastal salient of Pomerania"[45]. Churchill substantially agreed with the American position, although he seemed to favor allowing the Poles to take Silesia "as far as the Oder", if thereby he could obtain Soviet concessions allowing the London Poles' participation in the Lublin government, and that such annexations would not be more than the Poles could manage[46].

Still, Stalin favored Polish annexation of all territory up to the Oder and the Western Neisse Rivers, and pushed hard for this line throughout the Conference. He even mentioned that when he had met with Mikolajczyk in Moscow in late 1944 the latter had been delighted with the idea of a frontier on the Western Neisse River[47]. There seems to have been a hint

here that Stalin would recognize the authority of the London Poles, but only for certain concessions. The Americans and British came up with revised proposals for the boundary question, which Roosevelt read out near the end of the Conference. He stated: "no objection is perceived to the Soviet proposal that the eastern boundary of Poland should be the Curzon Line, with modifications in favour of Poland in some areas of from five to eight kilometres"[48]. This was readily agreed upon. As for the western frontier of Poland, Roosevelt proposed that Poland should receive "that portion of East Prussia south of the Königsberg line, Upper Silesia, and up to the line of the Oder; but there would appear to be little justification for extending it up to the Western Neisse."[49]

The Yalta Conference closed without further agreement being reached on the frontiers, although Stalin did agree that in exchange for the Oder Line concession, he would ensure the participation of the London Poles in the Lublin Government and free elections, despite Lublin's adament refusal to deal with the London Poles[50].

In the Report of the Crimea Conference, issued by the Big Three on February 11, 1945, the three powers agreed to deal with the Polish frontiers as follows:

> The three Heads of Government consider that the Eastern frontier of Poland should follow the Curzon Line with digressions from it in some regions of five to eight kilometres in favour of Poland. They recognize that Poland must receive substantial accessions of territory in the North and West. They feel that the opinion of the new Polish Provisional Government of National Unity should be sought in due course on the extent of these accessions and that **the final delimitation of the Western frontier of Poland should thereafter await the Peace Conference** (emphasis added).[51]

While few jurists consider that the Yalta statement has any more legal validity than the Teheran document, it is crucial for several reasons. First, while the statement more or less sets the definite line of the future Polish-Soviet frontier (legally or otherwise), it makes no definite statement about the future German-Polish frontier, although it does recognize the principle that Germany would have to cede some territory to Poland. However, this agreement to give "substantial accessions of territory" to Poland is held by Polish jurists to be binding upon the Yalta signatories[52]. On the other hand, some Western jurists dispute the notion that an agreement to either frontier was binding, or even legally valid. One writer stated shortly after the Yalta Conference:

> Why should "the three heads of government consider that the Eastern frontier of Poland should follow the Curzon line," when the existing frontier

> had been accepted by the U.S.S.R. by the Treaty of Riga of 1921, confirmed by the treaty of Non-agression of 1932, had been accepted by the United Kingdom by the decision of the Conference of Ambassadors of 1923 and had been accepted by the United States by Minister Gibson's note of 1923?...If the boundary of 1923 had been acceptable to the three Governments for over a score of years, why revert to a discredited "boundary?"[53]

This same writer went on to address the German-Polish frontier proposal:

> Is it an admission of guilt to recognize that by way of compensation "Poland must receive substantial accessions of territory in the North and West"? can one wrong done to an ally be righted by another wrong done to an enemy? Why be so definite in delimiting the eastern frontier and yet "feel...that the final delimitation of the western frontier of Poland should ...await the peace conference"?[54]

Most Polish sources do not attempt to find in the Yalta statement a clear and legally binding delimitation of the exact German-Polish frontier (although some may consider statements made during the conference as crucial to the interpretation of the guarantee of territory "in the north and west"). However, there is a strong argument made that some sort of substantial territorial grant was legally given at Yalta, and that future conference statements at Potsdam indicated exactly what territory had been guaranteed at Yalta[55]. In effect, Poles argue that once the Big Three had promised Poland German territory, this was binding upon all three powers under international law and future discussions could only define exact limits[56].

A second issue raised by the Yalta Declaration is the connection between a democratic government in Poland and the final German frontier. As mentioned earlier, the Western Allies seemed to hinge their acceptance of any substantial annexation of German territory on the democratic election of a government in Poland representative of all non-fascist parties. One of the greatest Polish authorities on the German-Polish frontier argues that the two issues have no valid connection under international law, and thus the Communist takeover in Poland in 1945, even if it violated the Soviet promise at Yalta to allow London Pole participation, would have no bearing on the frontier issue[57]. However, if the Yalta agreement has any validity in international law, a premise itself open to serious doubt[58], then the *entire* document must be valid, including the provisions relating to the formation of a Polish Provisional Government of all parties, and free and unfettered elections, neither of which ever took place.

How can proponents cite the territorial provisions agreed upon by the Big Three, yet ignore other provisions that were also agreed upon? In 1919 the victorious Allied powers would not have permitted Germany to agree to just some of the terms of the Treaty of Versailles, much less sign the Treaty and then choose to ignore most of its provisions (although this in fact occurred some years later, leading indirectly to World War Two).

The third aspect of the Yalta Declaration is the most vital for the subsequent disposition of the Oder-Neisse Territories. This involves the last phrase of the portion cited above, that "the final delimitation of the Western frontier of Poland should thereafter await the Peace Conference". This precise phrase was again used in the Potsdam Declaration (see below), and was the final statement made jointly by the Allied Powers after World War Two, in effect the latest and last evidence of the joint intentions of the Big Three. To most German writers this phrase was proof that no final determination had been made as to the German-Polish frontier. In the Yalta Declaration this distinction made little difference to most writers, as the Declaration made no specific mention of a possible western frontier in any case[59]. In the Potsdam Declaration, however, the fact that specific mention of the Oder and Western Neisse frontier was made seemed to some to give teeth to the argument that "final delimitation" only meant the technical survey of the new frontier, which allegedly was already established (see below). Thus a full discussion of this vital phrase must be reserved for the review of the Potsdam Declaration[60].

Following the Yalta Declaration the heads of the three Allied Powers made statements in their homelands that indicate how much of an agreement on the frontiers had *not* been reached. Churchill announced in the House of Commons on February 27, 1945:

> ...the three Powers have now agreed that Poland shall receive substantial accessions of territory both in the North and in the West. In the North she will certainly receive, in the place of the precarious Corridor, the great city of Danzig, the greater part of East Prussia West and South of Königsberg and a long, wide sea front on the Baltic. In the West she will receive the important industrial province of Upper Silesia and, in addition, such other territories to the East of the Oder as it may be decided at the peace settlement to detach from Germany after the views of a broadly based Polish Government have been ascertained...The Western frontiers...cannot be fixed except as part of the whole German settlement until ...after a fully representative Polish Government has been able to make its wishes known.[61]

Roosevelt made substantially the same claims, stating before Congress on March 1, 1945:

> the Poles will receive compensation in territory in the north and west in exchange for what they lose by the Curzon Line. The limits of the western boundary will be permanently fixed in the final peace conference.[62]

Stalin, on the other hand, was clear in his support of the Oder-Neisse frontier, and along with both the Lublin Poles and Mikolajczyk seemed to consider that all of the Yalta participants had agreed in principle to this line[63]. In support of their stand the Russians and Poles began installing Polish (or Russian) administrations in German territories east of the Oder-Neisse overrun by the Russian army between February and May, 1945. When the U.S. protested this action and the first expulsions of the German population, the Russians claimed the military necessity of installing Polish civilian government in the rear areas to safeguard supply lines and keep the occupied territories in order[64].

On June 5, 1945 Great Britain, the United States, the Soviet Union and France issued the Four Power Declaration and Statement Regarding Germany at Berlin. Article Two of the Declaration reads in part:

> (d) Evacuation by the said forces of all territories outside the frontiers of Germany **as they existed on the 31st December, 1937,** will proceed according to instructions to be given by the Allied Representatives[65] (emphasis added).

In the Statement regarding Germany is the clause reading:

> ...Germany, within her frontiers **as they were on 31st December, 1937**, will, for the purposes of occupation, be divided into four zones...[66] (emphasis added).

When, prior to the Potsdam Conference, the Soviets handed over most of the Oder-Neisse area to Polish administration, vigorous protests came from the U.S. and Great Britain[67]. This action was a blatant violation of the *specific* wording of the Berlin Declaration signed at precisely the same time that this action was in progress. As one scholar notes, "Not only was this a unilateral act and contrary to the agreement signed at Yalta, but it was also bound to complicate the problem of reparations"[68].

An important issue in post-surrender Germany was the power that the Allies had with respect to German territory and other legal matters. German proponents claim that the June 5th declaration was binding on

the Four Allies, thus prohibiting any actions inconsistent with the idea of Germany within her borders of 1937. More importantly, many find that the surrender of May 8, 1945 gave the Allies no rights except for occupation and the demobilization of the German armed forces. One U.S. congressman states: "The occupation did not effectuate a territorial change of title because, according to international law, the 'unconditional surrender' in 1945 of Germany was a military surrender. It was not a subjugation"[69]. This lawmaker goes on to argue that while international law holds conquest to be the basis for annexation, conquest is not completed until after a formal act of subjugation, such as the surrender of the German government, and Germany was never subjugated[70]. This argument fits well into the lack of a peace treaty, cited most often by German proponents and to be addressed in great detail below.

The Potsdam Conference, which took place between July 16 and August 1st, 1945 is held by many scholars as the conference that legally and permanently created the Oder-Neisse Line. In order to decide whether this is indeed the case, two issues must be resolved. First, is the Potsdam Declaration issued on August 1st a legally binding agreement, for the signatories and/or all parties affected by its terms? Second, did the Potsdam Declaration actually establish a frontier on the Oder-Neisse, or was this left indefinite or merely a temporary administrative situation?

As to the first issue, a great number of scholars, Polish, German and otherwise, recognize the Potsdam Declaration as a legally binding document. Others claim that it is merely a statement of intentions prior to a peace conference (like Teheran or Yalta), or instructions to the occupying forces[71]. One question, surprisingly not often raised, is whether the Potsdam Declaration could be considered a peace settlement. This seems improbable, in that the Declaration itself mentions "awaiting the peace settlement", and the fact that the defeated power did not negotiate or sign the document. After World War One an armistice was signed between the adversaries[72], as was done at Rheims on May 9th, 1945, that called for the withdrawl of German forces from occupied territory. Rheims also provided for the surrender of the German armed forces, but nothing more. After World War One no reparations, annexations, occupations or other actions were taken until after Germany had signed the Treaty of Versailles in 1919. In fact the Allied powers demanded that Germany sign the document or they would commence an invasion of Germany, and several German cabinets resigned before one finally agreed to sign the harsh terms[73]. If international law requires the term "peace treaty" to be strictly interpreted, then the terms of Potsdam may be mere verbiage. In 1926 the Permanent Court of International Justice held in one of its first opinions that until a treaty of peace had been concluded

between two states, the victorious state could take no action to annex territory or seize property within that territory, as for all purposes that territory remained under the jurisdiction of its former sovereign[74]. In that case (interestingly a dispute between the same two parties over the same territory), Poland had moved into German Upper Silesia in 1920, after the Treaty of Versailles but before the plebiscite scheduled for that area had taken place, and later expropriated German property. The Court held that Poland had no right to take this action until sovereignty had been officially handed over, even after the results of the plebiscite commission were announced, but before the official date of transfer of sovereignty. The most important language of the decision relates to the 1918 Armistice Convention, similar to the Potsdam Convention of 1945. The Court found that "the Armistice Convention did not possess the importance which Poland attempted to attribute to it", and was not in any way a peace treaty that would finalize a boundary. What this means for the Potsdam Declaration is that should it have been only the preliminary meeting for the future peace conference, it may be a legal nullity, and none of its provisions could be legally enforced. In fact, any action taken pursuant to the Potsdam Declaration would be, without more, a violation of international law[75].

As to the second issue, we must turn to an analysis of the Potsdam Conference and the intentions of the Big Three. At the beginning of the Potsdam Conference the three participants were quite obviously far apart in their attitudes towards the frontier issue, despite claims by Poland and the Soviet Union to the contrary. The United States delegation set out their ideas in a briefing book on July 4, 1945. The U.S. desired to give the Königsberg region of East Prussia to the Soviet Union, with the remainder to go to Poland. In addition, Danzig, Upper Silesia (the Oppeln District), and eastern Pomerania, defined as Pomerania east of a line running from Kreuz to Dramburg, would be transferred to Poland. The delegation specifically stated that all other territory east of the Oder, and especially the part of Silesia situated west of the Oder and Eastern Neisse Rivers, should remain German[76]. The British under Churchill considered that Yalta had only bound them to the Curzon Line as Poland's eastern frontier, subject to consultations with the Polish government, and to "substantial accessions of German territory" in the west, the precise territory to be determined at the peace conference[77]. The British specifically refused to see the frontier move further west than the Eastern Neisse in Silesia[78]. The Russian view was of course quite different. They considered that the Yalta Conference had definitely established the German-Polish frontier on the Oder and Western Neisse, and in fact their action in handing over the Oder-Neisse Territories to the Polish

administration even as their armies occupied them, for whatever reasons of military necessity, indicates this attitude[79].

The Potsdam delegates, now with Truman representing the United States and Churchill about to give up his place to Attlee, did not begin to seriously consider the Polish boundary question until almost the last week of July. At this time they heard from the new Polish government, represented by President Beirut, a long-time Communist. The entire Polish delegation was made up of members of the Lublin Communist group, except for the now powerless Mikolajczyk. They met first with the three foreign ministers, Molotov, Byrnes and Eden, on July 24th[80]. The Poles called for a new frontier on the Oder and Western Neisse, arguing that giving all of Silesia to Poland would help her industrially and deny the armaments industries to Germany, and that the Oder-Neisse frontier would be shorter and more easily defensible, and in any event would be minimal compensation for the loss of lands east of the Curzon Line[81]. Molotov of course readily supported this demand, citing especially the compensation necessary for the Curzon Line. Eden and Byrnes were non-committal. However, when the Poles presented their demands to the new Big Three, Churchill gave them an idea of where the Western Allies stood on the issue. He first stated that he was not in favor of Poland absorbing so much German land, especially when it meant expelling eight to ten million Germans. He then questioned the lack of free elections and of any democratic parties in Poland, which was a prerequisite for settling the Polish question, stating: "I did not believe that only Communists were democrats"[82]. Truman cut the Poles off short, stating that the border question "must be determined at the peace settlement"[83]. Stalin's statement of the Soviet position was rather surprising. When Truman stated that for the present time the term "Germany" should be considered the area within the frontiers of 1937, with which Churchill readily agreed, Stalin said that he "agreed that from a formal point of view Germany might be considered in this way", and furthermore he suggested that "the Western frontier of Poland be fixed now and that the question would then become clear"[84]. Stalin went on to agree that the frontiers of 1937 were a good starting point from which to discuss the frontier issue, and Churchill and Truman agreed[85]. Stalin's statement seems to contradict the previous positions indicated by Molotov and Marshall Zhukov, and clearly runs against the theory that the frontiers were finally established at Yalta, or any time prior to the Potsdam Conference.

On July 20 Molotov proposed to the other foreign ministers that "pending the final settlement of territorial questions at the Peace Congress, the western frontier of Poland to fix (sic) along the line marked on the attached map viz: west of Swinemunde to the river Oder leaving

Stettin on the Polish side, further up the river Oder to the estuary of the river West Neisse to the Czechoslovakian frontier"[86]. When this proposal reached the Big Three at their session on July 21 Churchill and Truman were adamantly opposed to the Western Neisse frontier, but seemed to be interested in a compromise on the rest, especially as to where the boundaries of zones of occupation would be drawn, and whether the Soviet zone would include areas east of the Oder-Neisse. In this area Stalin told Truman that everything he said was interpretive "since no frontiers had been ceded at the Crimea except for the provision that Poland would receive territory. The western frontier question is open and the Soviet Union is not bound"[87]. No compromise was ever forthcoming, however, and the Western Powers would remain adamantly opposed to the Western Neisse and, some argue, to anything past the pre-Potsdam position of East Prussia and Oppeln. On July 23 Stalin brought up the transfer of the Königsberg area to Russia, and neither Churchill nor Truman disagreed. They in fact agreed to support this proposal at the peace conference, although Truman said that "it would be necessary to study ethnographic and other questions", and that to formally promise cession of Königsberg to Russia "would also commit them to the recognition of the incorporation of Lithuania into the Soviet Union", and that these matters belonged to the final peace settlement[88].

On July 25 the Big Three discussed the proposed transfer of the German population from non-German areas, including territory to be ceded at the peace conference. This provision of the Potsdam Declaration is one kingpin of the argument that Potsdam did legally transfer the Oder-Neisse Territories to Poland and the Soviet Union, for why else would the Allies order the transfer of millions of German inhabitants from areas only under Polish-Soviet occupation[89]? This is a strong argument, and will be dealt with shortly. This was also the day that Mr. Attlee took over Mr. Churchill's office and his place at Potsdam. Churchill seems to have compromised somewhat in his position on Poland's western frontier, but still stated that he was opposed to Poland being allowed to seize, as it apparantly had, all German territory up to the Oder-Neisse, and the transfer of the German population prior to a peace settlement. Churchill was concerned about the economic ramifications, and said to the other delegates: "Much of Germany's grain came from the very land which the Poles had seized, and if this was denied us the Western Allies would be left with wrecked industrial zones and a starved and swollen population. For the future peace of Europe here was a wrong beside which Alsace-Lorraine and the Danzig Corridor were trifles"[90]. As to the Western Neisse Churchill was even more determined. Later he was to write: "I nor

Mr. Eden would ever have agreed to the Western Neisse being the frontier line. The line of the Oder and the Eastern Neisse had already been recognized as the Polish compensation for retiring to the Curzon Line..."[91]. In his memoirs Mr. Churchill wrote that when the Neisse question arose at Potsdam "I at once declared that Great Britain adhered only to the Eastern tributary. And this is still our position"[92].

The Soviets and Poles held firmly to their demands for the Oder-Neisse frontier. On July 30, only two days before the end of the Conference, U.S. Secretary of State Byrnes made a final compromise offer to Molotov to allow a "provisional" Polish administration up to the Western Neisse, pending a future treaty to settle the matter, and this proposal was accepted by Molotov[93]. Of course, by this time any agreement to allow a Polish administration in the Oder-Neisse Territories was only a legal nicety, for the Poles had long since taken over the area with Russian acquiescence, and had even begun to expel a large number of Germans (see below). When this compromise reached the Big Three it was accepted, whether out of a desperate desire to reach some sort of agreement it is not known. In deciding on the wording for their forthcoming declaration, Truman followed the advice of Harry Hopkins, Stettinius and others in the delegation in refusing to agree specifically to the Oder-Neisse as the final frontier change, although he did agree to address the Curzon Line in the east as a definite decision, contrary to his advisors' wishes[94]. With respect to the Königsberg Territory the Russians wished to delete any wording that would make the transfer provisional and subject to the peace settlement, but Byrnes insisted that the language not indicate "an immediate transfer of territory", and Molotov agreed with a British proposal to include a commission of experts at the peace conference to finally determine the extent of the Königsberg cession to the Soviet Union[95].

The Potsdam Declaration, signed by Truman, Stalin and Attlee and announced on August 2nd, 1945, contains three sections dealing with the Oder-Neisse Territories. Section VI is entitled "City of Königsberg and the Adjacent Area", Section IX is entitled "Poland" and Section XIII "Orderly Transfers of German Populations". The first two are key to the boundary problem itself, while the third will be addressed mainly in the chapter of this work pertaining to the expellees, with the exception of its use by some scholars to give weight to their arguments for the finality of the new frontiers.

Section VI, Königsberg, reads as follows:

> The Conference examined a proposal by the Soviet Government that pending the final determination of territorial questions at the peace

> settlement, the section of the western frontier of the Union of Soviet Socialist Republics which is adjacent to the Baltic Sea should pass from a point on the eastern shore of the Bay of Danzig to the east, north of Braunsberg-Goldap, to the meeting point of the frontiers of Lithuania, the Polish Republic and East Prussia.
>
> The Conference has agreed in principle to the proposal of the Soviet Government concerning the ultimate transfer to the Soviet Union of the City of Königsberg and the area adjacent to it as described above subject to expert examination of the actual frontier.
>
> The President of the United States and the British Prime Minister have declared that they will support the proposal of the Conference at the forthcoming peace settlement.[96]

What is most notable about this particular agreement is that it is very definite, as is the Curzon Line provision in Section XIII (see below). While there is the qualification "pending the final determination of territorial questions", there is here even a specific guarantee from the Western Powers of support for the annexation at the peace conference. As Poland and the Soviet Union would certainly support this action, and France bound herself to the decisions of the Potsdam Conference[97], it is clear that all of the concerned parties were in agreement on Königsberg, and had a peace conference been held, barring some unforeseen split between the Allies this transfer would have been part of any treaty. Outside of a treaty signed with Germany transferring this land, however, was there any justification for the Russian annexation of Königsberg?

The two major reasons put forth by the Russians for their desire for Königsberg were the need for an ice-free port and the justice, after four years of brutal war against the Germans, of annexing at least a small piece of German territory, especially the historic capital of one of the oldest parts of Prussia. There was no attempt, as the Poles did, to justify the annexation on grounds of ethnicity or historic claims. As one writer states: "The Russians never attempted historic and/or ethnic rationalisation, because they could not...the population was not akin to any of the peoples of the USSR"[98]. As we have seen, Russia has no historic ground for demanding the Königsberg area. Neither the Soviet Union nor its historic or ethnic predecessors, indeed no Slav nation, has ever occupied northern East Prussia, which has one of the simplest ethnic histories in the region. Neither the Russians nor the Poles are successors to either the Prussians or the Germans, the only two peoples to occupy northern East Prussia in recorded history. The argument for an ice-free port, undoubtedly an attempt at greater security, seems more justified[99]. The area of northern

East Prussia is not large, and would not have seemed too large of a claim for the Soviet Union after that nation had suffered so terribly at the hands of the Germans between 1941 and 1945. The problem is that such an annexation, unless qualified by other provisions in a treaty, would of necessity recognize the Soviet annexation of Lithuania, which was never addressed by the Allied Powers in any conference, or by any subsequent treaty. The wording that spells doom to Lithuania is that specifying that the Soviet frontier was to run along a line from the Bay of Danzig to the Polish-Lithuanian-East Prussian frontier. If northern East Prussia, known to the Lithuanians as Lithuania Minor, was to be an isolated territory of the Soviet Union as East Prussia had been to Germany before 1939, separated from the motherland by the territory of another state, then the wording of the article should have mentioned that the border also ran along the Niemen River, or along the old East Prussian frontier, etc. The fact that the parties to the Potsdam Conference failed to take into account Lithuania may nullify the Russian annexation of Königsberg. It would be very difficult to argue that the provisions of the Atlantic Charter do not apply to the Baltic States, which were some of the first victims of Nazi-Soviet aggression in 1940. The Russian annexation was certainly not welcomed by a majority of the Lithuanian population. The Lithuanians, along with most minorities in the Soviet Union, greeted the invading German Army in 1941 as a liberator, and even after World War Two the Lithuanians carried on a guerilla war against the Russians until the 1950s[100]. Thus if the Atlantic Charter is applied to Lithuania, the Russian occupation would be a nullity and Russian Königsberg would be inconveniently isolated from the rest of the Soviet Union[101]. As Sharp has stated, the Russian claim to Königsberg was "an act of pure annexation in the Great Power tradition."[102]

The more important aspect of Article VI is that the Conference agreed to "the **ultimate** transfer" of Königsberg "subject to expert examination of the actual frontier" (emphasis added). The wording would seem to be self-explanatory. The intention of Potsdam was to transfer Königsberg to Russia only at the time of the peace conference. Thus it would legally not belong to Russia until that time, although occupied by Russian troops. While unlike the Oder-Neisse Line the transfer of Königsberg was almost inevitable under the Potsdam agreement, and its exact limits were more or less defined (as with the Curzon Line), it could no more be considered as having been transferred at Potsdam than any other territory (the arguments on this point will be dealt with in more detail below). The wording of Article VI may be more specific than Article IX dealing with the Oder-Neisse, but it ultimately left the final determination to the peace conference.

Article IX entitled "Poland" deals with two aspects of the problem, the Polish provisional government and the frontiers. After noting the Three Powers' recognition of the Polish Provisional Government, the Article goes on to state:

> The three Powers note that the Polish Provisional Government in accordance with the decisions of the Crimea Conference has agreed to the holding of free and unfettered elections as soon as possible on the basis of universal suffrage and secret ballot in which all democratic and anti-Nazi parties shall have the right to take part and to put forward candidates....[103]

As to the western frontier of Poland the Article reads:

> The three Heads of Government reaffirm their opinion that the final limitation of the western frontier of Poland should await the peace settlement.
>
> The three Heads of Government agree that, pending the final determination of Poland's western frontier, the former German territories east of a line running from the Baltic Sea immediately west of Swinemunde, and thence along the Oder River to the confluence of the western Neisse River and along the western Neisse to the Czechoslovak frontier, including that portion of East Prussia not placed under the administration of the Union of Soviet Socialist Republics in accordance with the understanding reached at this conference and including the area of the former free city of Danzig, shall be under the administration of the Polish State and for such purposes should not be considered as part of the Soviet zone of occupation in Germany.[104]

This most crucial article is used by both proponents and opponents of the Oder-Neisse Line to prove their arguments, such is its ambiguity. We shall review the territorial provisions first.

The Poles argue that this article gave the precise territories outlined in it to Poland outright. The "final determination" or "final limitation" of the frontier means nothing more than precise surveys and demarcation. This argument is best expressed by Boleslaw Wiewiora, who argues that there are four main stages in settling state frontiers. These include political decisions, delimitation in a treaty "or other official document", demarcation on the spot, and administration of the boundary[105]. Wiewiora argues that Potsdam legally accomplished the first two elements, so that all that was left for the peace conference was the technical survey. As we shall see, many argue that even this part of the process was legally accomplished by East Germany and Poland in 1950 with the Treaty of Gorlitz. Adding weight to this argument is the phrase used in the Article identifying the lands in question as "the former German territories". Few

proponents of the finality of the Line fail to stress this phrase[106]. Accompanied by the expulsions of Germans authorized by Article XIII, this is truly a powerful argument. However, if the entire arrangement was provisional, and dependent upon the final peace settlement, then the exact "former German territories" would have to be defined at that time, and until then the Western Allies capitulated to the de facto situation of Polish-Soviet occupation of all lands under consideration for annexation. This argument has considerable viability when considering the events of the last week at Potsdam, outlined above. One German writer asserts that the fact that the territories were only placed under the "administration" of Poland was an indication that "final delimitation" meant more than a technical survey. To support this he cites a declaration submitted by U.S. Secretary Byrnes on July 31, accepted by all members of the Conference, that "By this action the Three Powers agreed to the administration in the interim by Poland..."[107].

Western writers indicate that "delimitation" is not simply a technical action. Dr. F.K. Menon states that "delimitation means the choice of a boundary site and its definition in a treaty or agreement", while "demarcation", a term *not* used in the Potsdam Agreement, is the "actual tracing of the boundary by a commission after the coming into force of the treaty"[108]. These concepts were applied by the International Court of Justice in a similar but smaller frontier dispute between Belgium and the Netherlands[109]. In that case the two states argued over the applicability of the Treaty of London, which formalised the separation of the two countries in 1839. The Treaty specified that the exact boundary would be "delimited" by a boundary commission after the Treaty was signed. The Treaty itself contained specifications as to which territory would be granted to each party, but the final boundary commission's delimitation varied with the Treaty provisions in some areas. The Court held that only the territorial settlement reached after *delimitation* was applicable, and not the provisions of the separation treaty[110].

One aspect of the Article cited often by German proponents is that the territories were "placed under the administration" of Poland or the Soviet Union, not 'ceded' to or 'annexed' by them. It is nearly impossible to argue that placing territory of one state under the 'administration' of another is the same thing as outright annexation. If the Potsdam delegates had intended to cause the Oder-Neisse Territories to be annexed by Poland and the Soviet Union, why did they not use this or a similar term in the Declaration? In fact, allowing Poland to "administer" the German lands east of the Oder-Neisse conforms with the original Soviet argument put forth at Potsdam to explain why the Soviets had established Polish administrations in these areas prior to the Potsdam Conference, namely

for strategic reasons and due to a lack of sufficient Soviet personnel to handle local administration (see above). While the Oder-Neisse Territories may not have been in the same status as the four military occupation zones in Germany, they were "administrative" districts as opposed to territory completely handed over to a new power[111]. This is a recognized type of legal entity in international law. The oldest known example of a territory being placed under the "administration" of another state while still technically under the sovereignty of the first state is in the Treaty of Berlin signed in 1878 between the major powers of Europe to settle Balkan affairs. In Article XXV the Turkish provinces of Bosnia and Herzegovina were placed under the "administration" of Austria-Hungary[112]. Notably, Austria-Hungary had wanted to annex the Provinces outright, but the other conferees, especially Russia, feared that this would give Austria too much influence in the Balkans. When in 1908 Austria-Hungary unilaterally declared the outright annexation of Bosnia-Herzegovina there were strong protests from other states, and tensions rose in the Balkans. In the Sinai Peninsula the Ottoman Empire granted to Egypt the right to administer the southern part of the peninsula in 1892, and this situation was confirmed with Great Britain, the occupant of Egypt, in 1906. However, when Egypt attempted to claim this territory in later years legal authorities denied that Egypt had valid title to sovereignty of the Peninsula. As Whiteman notes:

> The case of Egypt and its rights over the Sinai Peninsula would seem to fall squarely within the limits of (the doctrine of) "Cession of Administration," by which the ceding State retains all of its rights of sovereignty over the conceded lands and confers nothing more than the mere administration of the territory concerned. Such was the case, for example, of the Convention between Turkey and Austria, in 1879, for the administration of Bosnia and Herzegovina.[113]

In 1951, when the Oder-Neisse controversy was still a central issue, the British M.P. Mr. Fitzroy McLean stated in the House of Commons during debate over the Sinai Question: "Surely the mere fact of administration does not confer sovereignty"[114]. Is there any reason to believe that the question would not also apply to the Oder-Neisse Territories?

There are several other examples of the territory of one state being "administered" by another state. A border region between Egypt and Sudan includes some desert land east of Lake Nasser within the frontiers of Sudan, but is recognized as administered by Egypt (unfortunately, no scholastic writing has appeared on this situation but the Egyptian-Sudanese situation was apparantly created by mutual consent). The island

of Cyprus, controlled by Turkey for hundreds of years, was occupied by the British in 1878. However, not until the Treaty of Lausanne in 1923 was sovereignty renounced in favor of Great Britain. In the Pacific Ocean, the Japanese-owned Ryukyu and Bonin Islands were put under the "administration" of the United States by the Treaty of San Francisco in 1951, and were properly returned to full Japanese sovereignty in 1968[115]. In the north of Japan, the Soviet Union still occupies four islands in the Kurile chain that were Japanese before the War. As no treaty has been signed between the Soviet Union and Japan, the Japanese and much of the World still consider the islands "occupied", and the Russians and Japanese are indeed negotiating for the return of these islands now under Soviet "administration"[116]. Of course the most well-known example of lands under hostile "administration" are the West Bank and Gaza Strip of Palestine/Israel. Most states and the United Nations have denounced the Israeli occupation as illegal, and do not recognize her unilateral annexation of Jerusalem. As recently as July, 1988 the King of Jordan re-asserted his sovereignty over the West Bank by declaring it an independent state, pending its "liberation" from Israeli "occupation".

These examples show that the term "administration" means something less than outright annexation, and if that term can be differentiated in 1878 and again in 1988, then it must have meant something other than annexation in 1945. The Permanent Court of International Justice addressed the issue in 1937 when it held that the Turkish islands of Crete and Samos, occupied by Great Britain in 1913, remained under Turkish sovereignty until the Treaty of Lausanne finally transferred them to Greece in 1923, even though the Turks practically exercised no authority on the islands after 1913[117]. One scholar terms this situation "residual sovereignty"[118]. However little actual authority or control the first state exercises over the territory, that territory remains under the sovereignty of the first nation until a valid treaty transfers such sovereignty.

Some writers point out that the Oder-Neisse Territories were rapidly integrated with the rest of Poland, and on November 13, 1945 Poland passed a decree extending Polish law and administrative regions over the territories. The Polish Ministry of the Recovered Territories was a transitional administrative organ of the Polish government[119]. This action only indicates Poland's attitude towards the legal status of the Territories, which was already well known. The domestic actions of one state do not prove the legality of an international action, but only their intentions behind it. Other writers argue that the term "administration" was not incompatible with a frontier decision that was not subject to revision. They state that "administration" was only a formal term used to indicate that

the territorial changes were subject to final confirmation at a peace conference, but did not mean that they were temporary[120].

The first part of Article IX, relating to free elections and democratic parties, was cited often in later years by the Western Allies and their proponents to support their common-law contract interpretation of the Potsdam Declaration[121]. This argument maintains that since Poland failed to ever hold "free and unfettered elections" and in fact suppressed all but the Communist Party, it violated, along with the Soviet Union, the provisions of Article IX. Therefore it could not take advantage of other parts of the Article, as Poland and Russia had voided all privileges under the Potsdam Declaration. By common-law standards, this meant that a violation of one provision of the contract allowed the other parties to void the contract. While common law is not part of international law, a similar principle of fairness should follow that would forbid a party to any international agreement from only selectively following the provisions of that agreement. German writers also stress this Polish inconsistency in following the dictates of the Potsdam Declaration. Meyer-Lindenberg writes that "Section I(A) with regard to the creation of a free and democratic system of government stands in a reciprocal relationship to the rights which were conceded to Poland under (B) with regard to the exercise of administrative authority in the eastern German territories"[122]. As Potsdam was only a preliminary agreement setting out the intentions of the parties for the peace conference, one can speculate that Polish violations of Article IX would lead the Western Powers to seriously reconsider whether they wished to hand over to a Poland governed by a one-party dictatorship (and placed in power by the Soviet Army) a great amount of German land. Thus whether Potsdam was a final settlement or whether it was a preliminary outline for the peace conference, the Soviet-Polish violation of Article IX (A) would drastically effect its outcome, and most likely void any territorial transfer.

One of the strongest arguments for the permanent character of the Potsdam decision regarding the frontiers is Article XIII, authorizing the orderly transfer of German populations from Poland, Czechoslovakia and Hungary. Russian writers consider this point as conclusive and that "a final understanding had been reached in principle in Potsdam"[123]. Some Western writers agree, and cite also the fact that Potsdam placed no limit on the type of resettlement or reconstruction that Poland could undertake in these territories[124]. From a German domestic standpoint, the expellees were quickly assimilated into the devastated west and even in Germany apparantly lost much of their identity, despite the fact that they had numbered over ten million in the late 1940s. By 1957 their political party, the BHE, won scarcely 5% of the vote[125]. However, the exact wording of

Article XIII allows transfers from "Poland". As the frontiers were only to be finally determined at the peace conference, it was uncertain at the time of the expulsions exactly where the state of Poland was located in its western area. This Article could very well have authorized the transfer of Germans settled in pre-1939 Poland and those brought in during the War, but not the millions inhabiting eastern Germany[126].

One theory advanced by German scholars to disclaim the Potsdam Agreement entirely is that of "res inter alios gesta", that an agreement between several states that is not addressed to the affected state (Germany) can not affect that state. This theory, when taken to its limits, supports the contention that the Allies could not speak for Germany in matters of territorial cession although they were in complete occupation of the country[127]. Along with this argument the Germans claim that the rights of the Allies with respect to Germany are derived from the Berlin Declaration of June 5, 1945 and not from the Potsdam Declaration[128]. Polish proponents refute both of these arguments. Firstly, the Potsdam Declaration is not "res inter alios gesta" because the Declaration, Article II specifically addresses the German people and the intention of the Allied Powers to help them rebuild and become a peaceful nation. Secondly, the claim that the Potsdam Declaration is not binding upon Germany would seriously challenge the absolute right of the Allies to decide the fate of Germany[129]. The German argument appears invalid when we see that international law does not recognize the principle of "pacta tertiis nec nocent nec prosunt", or one state can not determine the rights and duties of another[130]. Thus, Germany would seem to be bound by the Potsdam Declaration even though she was not a party to it[131]. If this is indeed the case, than state practice in recent history has not followed this norm of international law. Every major European war of the last three centuries prior to World War Two has been concluded with a peace treaty, and a good number have also been immediately terminated by an armistice. As we saw above, even the Austrian cession of Silesia to Prussia in 1742 was accomplished by two peace treaties. The conclusion of World War One only twenty-six years before Potsdam belies the argument that an armistice will act as the equivalent of a peace treaty. Germany signed an armistice with the Entente powers on November 11, 1918 in a railroad car in the Argonne Forest. At this time no German territory was occupied by Allied troops (except for a small part of Alsace), and the German army was still in the field. The German army was required to withdraw inside the frontiers of Germany as of 1914. German administration remained in all of the territories under German suzereignty in 1914 until the Treaty of Versailles had been signed in 1919. Although the Treaty of Versailles called for cession of large territories to Poland, the holding of plebiscites,

the cession of Alsace-Lorraine to France and the occupation of part of Germany by French troops, none of this was undertaken until the Germans had sent a government delegation to sign the Treaty[132]. In fact, when most members of the German government, as well as the German populace, refused to agree to the harsh terms of Versailles and several cabinets resigned rather than sign the document, the Entente forces threatened to continue the war. At no time, however, did they try to implement the terms of the Treaty until it had been signed[133]. When the German armies had retired into Germany per the armistice terms of November 11, the Allied armies could have followed them in and occupied Germany, but they did not, and instead waited for the Treaty to be signed. Likewise, in 1945 the German armed forces signed an armistice at Rheims (and later in Berlin for the benefit of the Russians). It is true that most of Germany had been conquered by the Allies and was under occupation. However, the German armies were still in the field in Bavaria, Austria, Bohemia and a large portion of coastal northern Germany and still controlled all of Denmark and Norway. A German government was active in Flensberg. The German military situation in May, 1945 was hopeless but not yet finished. Thus a situation on par with that of 1918 was again present in 1945, and if it took a Treaty in 1919 to pass legal title of territory from one state to another, than the same should hold true in 1945. Furthermore, the Permanent Court of International Justice specifically recognized this principle in the Case of Certain German Interests in Polish Upper Silesia, which did not allow Polish seizure of property in lands granted to Poland until they had legally passed as set by the Treaty and subsequent plebiscite agreements[134]. Thus, the statement by one writer that "in general, armistice terms seem to be controlling with regard to territorial decisions"[135] is not supported by facts. Professor Alfons Klafkowski has outlined four ways in which hostilities may be terminated and territorial questions settled. The first "and most often practised" way is by a peace treaty, another is by a unilateral declaration by one belligerant[136]. A third way described by Klafkowski is "debellatio", or total destruction of the enemy state[137], also known as conquest or subjugation. Many writers claim that this was the condition of Germany in May, 1945, but facts show otherwise. As previously noted, large areas of central and northern Europe were still occupied by German troops and a fully functional German government was operating in Flensberg, still in German territory. German government and military representatives chose to surrender to the Allies on May 8th to avoid further useless bloodshed, but the war could have been carried on for a considerably longer period, especially in mountainous Bavaria and Norway. This situation contrasts sharply with Belgium and the Netherlands in 1940, or Poland in 1939,

which were completely overrun by the invading armies and totally occupied, and their armed forces cleared from the field. Yet even in these extreme cases peace treaties were not signed with the defeated governments, which fled into exile, and thus no nation outside of the Axis orbit recognized territorial changes. Even had Germany fallen under the concept of "debellatio", in most cases "theory rejects 'the law of the conqueror'", and thus total subjugation of Germany prior to surrender would probably not have affected the territorial outcome[138]. This disproves the oft-claimed maxim that 'to the victor belong the spoils', and comports with the Atlantic Charter and the spirit of the U.N. Charter.

The last method of terminating a war according to Klafkowski is the situation found in 1945, namely the cession of hostilities on both sides without any definite understanding as to the legal results of this state. Klafkowski admits that the legal ramifications of this outcome remain uncertain, as this has rarely occurred, but his opinion is that in such a case the principle of "uti possidetis" prevails with regard to territorial questions, which means that the parties are to retain possession of what they have acquired by force during the war[139]. The only problem with this solution is that it encourages territorial conquest and discourages the conclusion of peace treaties or peaceful settlement of disputes, and thereby runs against the proscription against taking territory by force embodied in the Atlantic Charter and the U.N. Charter. What the Germans are really saying was first enunciated by the Roman writer Titus Pomponius: "Id quod nostrum est, sine facto nostro ad alium transferri non potest"[140]. Thus mere military occupation will not lead to annexation without a formal peace treaty in which the defeated power signs over title of territory to another power.

If state recognition of territorial changes is a requisite to the legality of such changes[141], the official statements of two of the three governments that signed the Potsdam Declaration indicate that the territorial provisions were not considered permanent until the peace conference. On October 10, 1945 British Secretary of State Bevin stated in the House of Commons that "His Majesty's Government are in no way committed to support the existing provisional arrangements at the Peace Conference"[142]. In November the U.S. issued a statement of its official policy with regard to Germany and specified that "The frontiers of Germany are for the present to be considered as those of January 1, 1938..."[143]. In 1946 U.S. Secretary of State Byrnes made his famous speach at Stuttgart in which he emphasized that the Oder-Neisse Territories were only placed provisionally under the administration of Poland and the Soviet Union, and even went so far as to say that "the heads of government did not agree to support at the peace settlement the cession of this particular area"[144].

Even French Minister of Foreign Affairs Bidault remarked that France could not understand the cession of a wholly German city like Königsberg to Russia, which had no historic or ethnic claim, and France would have to make reservations to her accession to the Potsdam Agreement, as the Oder-Neisse Line would set the center of gravity of Germany too far west[145]. Interestingly, even the Soviet Union and Poland did not appear to consider the Potsdam Agreement at first as a permanent settlement of the boundary question. On August 16th, 1945 these two states concluded a treaty relating to the Polish-Soviet state frontier[146]. While Articles 1 and 2 deliniate the Curzon Line in great detail, Article 3 reads as follows:

> **Until such time as territorial questions have been finally decided by peaceful settlement**, the part of the Polish-Soviet frontier adjoining the Baltic Sea shall, in accordance with the decision taken at the Berlin Conference, follow a line starting from a point on the Eastern shore of the Gulf of Danzig, indicated on the attached map, continuing in an easterly direction north of Braunsberg-Goldap, to the point where that line meets the frontier line described in Article 2 of the present Treaty[147] (emphasis added).

The wording of Article 3 contradicts the statements made by Polish and Soviet statesmen and scholars, especially in later years, about the finality of the changes allegedly made at Potsdam. This also belies the argument that Potsdam was itself a peace treaty. A peace treaty may only be concluded with the vanquished power, and occupied Germany did not, and could not, sign the Potsdam Protocol, and thus was not a party to its terms[148].

The Great Powers met to attempt to resolve the boundary dispute for the last time in 1947, at the Foreign Ministers' Meetings in Moscow and London. No ground was won or lost by either side, and while the U.S. and Great Britain continued to maintain that the Oder-Neisse Line was temporary, pending final decisions at a peace conference, Poland and the Soviet Union argued that it was permanent, and France, while disagreeing with the cession of so much land that would force the Germans to live in a much smaller area, acted as a mediator in the hopes of reaching some agreement on the subject. No such agreement emerged[149]. In the wake of the unsuccessful Foreign Ministers' Meetings the Soviet Union and Poland set up the Mixed Polish-Soviet Commission for the Demarcation of the State Frontier, the result being signed at Warsaw on April 30, 1947. Shortly thereafter (1948) the two nations concluded a new frontier treaty that stated in Article 1 that the Treaty of August 16, 1945 had established the new state frontier and that this had been demarcated by the

Commission in 1947 [150]. Interestingly, while in both the 1945 and 1948 Polish-Soviet treaties the Curzon Line and its slight deviations in favor of Poland is described in great detail up to the Polish-Lithuanian-East Prussian frontier, the line dividing East Prussia is never detailed, and the annexes to the 1948 Treaty include a protocol describing the Polish-Soviet frontier from the Czechoslovak frontier to the Lithuanian-East Prussian frontier, but no document describing the dividing line of East Prussia from Lithuania to the Bay of Danzig. The deliberate vagueness in the Treaties with regard to the East Prussian frontier is hard to explain, unless this is another indication that the Soviets and Poles still considered the matter unsettled.

The Cold War between the Western Powers and the Soviet Union ended any chance that a mutually agreeable solution to the German problem, including reunification and boundaries, would be forthcoming. In 1949 the American, British and French zones of occupation were combined to create the Federal Republic of Germany (BRD) with a constitution based upon principles of the Western democracies. The Soviet Union refused to join its zone to this state, and shortly after created the German Democratic Republic (DDR) out of its zone of occupation. As the Soviets and Poles had considered the Oder-Neisse Territories as having been effectively annexed at the latest at the time of Potsdam, there was no question of including them even provisionally in the territory of the German Democratic Republic[151]. The next year this situation was confirmed in a treaty between Poland and the D.D.R. This treaty, "wishing to stabilize and strengthen mutual relations on the basis of the Potsdam Agreement, which established the frontier on the Oder and Western Neisse", and "recognizing the established and existing frontier as an inviolable frontier", states in Article 1:

> The High Contracting Parties concur in confirming that the established and existing frontier, running from the Baltic Sea along a line to the west of the inhabited locality of Swinoujscie and thence along the Oder River to the confluence of the Western Neisse and along the Western Neisse to the Czechoslovak frontier, is the State frontier between Poland and Germany.[152]

Article 3 goes on to create a mixed commission "for the purpose of demarcating on the ground the Polish-German State frontier referred to in article 1..."[153]. The parties seem to have intended that this treaty would establish the permanent frontier on the Oder-Neisse, as there was no question of this treaty being "provisional". There is some room for argument against this interpretation, however. In 1946 Wilhelm Pieck,

head of the German Communist Party and first president of the D.D.R, stated that he could not accept the Oder-Neisse Line as the definitive boundary. Later East German domestic laws pertaining to boundary regulations treated the Polish frontier as a "special frontier" like that with the B.R.D, regulated as with internal travel. Only much later was it "normalized" and travel restrictions eased[154]. The great question that was brought out by the Gorlitz Agreement is whether the D.D.R. had the power and authority to conclude a boundary treaty binding upon itself or any other state, especially the B.R.D, and whether the D.D.R. is a legal entity in the international sphere at all. For this analysis we will have to discuss the legal status of post-1945 Germany in general.

As an aside before we enter this analysis, it is interesting to note that the D.D.R. signed its first treaty with the Soviet Union in 1955. Nowhere in this agreement are boundaries even mentioned, nor are they mentioned in any subsequent agreements[155]. Thus any legal changes such treaties may bring, as discussed below, will have no affect on the Königsberg Territory, occupied by the Soviet Union.

The basic tenets of the arguments with respect to the Gorlitz Agreement are simple. The Poles contend that the German Democratic Republic was a sovereign independent state in 1950, able to conclude international agreements and transfer territory at will. The D.D.R. was bound, as were all other concerned parties, by the Potsdam Agreement, and even had the Gorlitz Treaty not been signed, the status of the Oder-Neisse Territories would be the same. The West Germans, however, argue that the D.D.R. was not a sovereign state capable of concluding any sort of international agreement, but was still merely the Soviet-occupied sector of Germany. The West German argument is more complex in that it holds, pursuant to B.R.D. official policy, that the B.R.D. is the one and only successor of pre-1945 Germany. In fact a united Germany never ceased to exist, but was merely occupied for a time, with eastern and central Germany still under (illegal) occupation. As such, any frontier agreement must be concluded with a united Germany, or possibly with the B.R.D. as the representative of Germany. Of course the D.D.R. did not recognize the B.R.D.'s status as the continuation of the German Reich, although the D.D.R. was willing from the start to recognize the B.R.D. as another sovereign German state, just like herself, even though the B.R.D. would never consider recognizing the D.D.R. While this situation has changed somewhat over the years, especially after 1970, the philosophy and practice even today are more similar to those of 1950 than many people realize.

The foreign policy of the B.R.D. was dominated from 1949 to the mid-1960s by the administration of Chancellor Konrad Adenauer, who saw the B.R.D. rebuilt from the destruction of war to the new "Wirtschaftwunder"

in scarcely ten years. Adenauer had no intention of recognizing the Oder-Neisse Line, and there was a significant amount of political preasure in West Germany from the Expellee Associations ("Landsmannschaften") and other groups to support this way of thinking. Germans were dominated during the Cold War by the threat of the Soviet "Empire", especially after West Germany was rearmed and joined N.A.T.O. in 1955. West Germany's order of priority for foreign policy goals was "security, preservation of peace, and reunification"[156]. While Adenauer felt that detente was the only immediate way to maintain peace and allow Germany to rebuild, he was very mistrustful of the West's attempts at detente with the Soviet Union, fearing that any agreement might lead to the West abandoning West Germany, and thus withdrawing support for the (West) German claim to the Oder-Neisse Territories[157]. While Adenauer was a traditional German believer in "Realpolitik", and shared the German desire for reunification, his actions were forced by the circumstances of the Cold War to be blended with general Western or N.A.T.O. policies, and thus Germany's attitude toward Poland and the Soviet Union must be seen as reflecting Western attitudes in general[158]. Put another way, Western attitudes towards the occupants of the Oder-Neisse Territories conformed closely to those of the B.R.D.

Numerous German theorists argue that Adenauer's position was a legal as well as political stand. Especially with regard to the legal status of the two Germanies, many scholars in the West supported him. As to the argument that Germany ceased to exist in 1945, one writer states:

> Between 1945 and 1949 Germany's legal status was centred around the fundamental fact, established by the Declaration of Berlin of June 5, 1945...that neither Germany as a whole nor any part of it had, as a result of the surrender and the occupation, come under the sovereignty of another State, for the Four Governments expressly disclaimed any intention of annexation...They confined themselves to assuming "supreme authority with respect to Germany". This meant governmental authority, not a condominium, but a coimperium.[159]

Mann writes that while the occupation authorities set up in Germany were governments of the occupation powers modelled after their own systems, and often staffed by occupation personnel, they were not tied in to the occupying powers' home governments. Specific examples used by Mann include the courts, which although headed by Americans, British, etc. were the highest authority, and decisions could not be appealed to a U.S. or British high court[160]. The same structure existed in the bureacracy, at least in the three western zones. As Mann states: "The underlying idea of all

these complicated arrangements undoubtedly was that Germany as a State, though not as a sovereign State, continued to exist, and that it remained a single, unitary State, though it was governed by **five** different governmental authorities" (emphasis added) [161]. German writers argue that the old Reich still exists in the form of the B.R.D. The only way that it could have ceased to exist would be through debellatio or subjugation, and according to this school of thought neither of these eventualities occurred, as the Berlin Declaration of June 5th, 1945 expressly declared that the military occupation would not affect annexation[162]. The argument continues that such annexation could only take place through a treaty concluded with "an all-German Government", as expressly confirmed by the Potsdam delegates[163]. The drawback to this line of reasoning is that if West Germany was only a provisional state, awaiting the reunification of Germany, then it might not be recognized as the de jure government of Germany and have no more status in international law than East Germany[164]. If neither state has any status in international law, then the four occupying powers would retain ultimate control, especially in international relations. This situation seems to be confirmed by the fact that when the Occupation Statute, giving a considerable amount of control over German affairs to the Allied powers even after the B.R.D. was created, came to an end in 1955, it was superseded by the Convention on Relations between the Three Powers and the Federal Republic of Germany, signed in Paris on October 23, 1954 [165]. This Convention specifically reserved to the three Western occupation powers "the rights and responsibilities heretofore exercised or held by them relating to Berlin and to Germany as a whole, including the reunification of Germany and a peace settlement"[166]. An indication that the three Western powers were indeed of the opinion that only a united Germany could settle the frontier issue is shown by three identical notes submitted by the U.S., France and Great Britain to the Soviet Government on March 25, 1952. Each stated that: "In its view, it will not be possible to engage in detailed discussion of a peace treaty until conditions have been created for free elections and until a free all-German Government which could participate in such discussion has been formed". All concluded that "the final determination of territorial questions must await the peace settlement"[167]. Even the Soviet Union showed a desire for a reunified Germany. Foreign Minister Molotov stated several years before: "We are naturally in principle in favor of concluding a peace treaty with Germany; but before such a treaty can be concluded **a single German Government must be formed...**"(emphasis added)[168]. Thus all four powers with authority over Germany agreed that a peace treaty could only be concluded once Germany had been reunited and one government formed. Without a

peace treaty a permanent territorial settlement would not be possible, a fact recognized by the same four powers (see above). It is rather inexplicable how the Soviet Union could recognize the territorial settlement of Gorlitz. In fact, the three Western Powers, and the vast majority of members of the United Nations, refused to recognize the D.D.R., and it remained an isolated state, or entity, in international law for years. For some theorists, this lack of recognition is the final element that proves that "the German Democratic Republic is not a State and does not exist"[169]. If this is indeed true, then the conclusions become simple. As Dr. Mann aptly summarizes:

> Germany is still a single, undivided, unitary State. It has not suffered any dismemberment or loss of territory...who could possibly have acquired sovereignty over the Eastern territories. Certainly not the 'German Democratic Republic', for it does not exist as a State. Certainly not the Soviet Union, for not even the Four Allies jointly annexed Germany in 1945...Therefore, no State other than Germany can lay claim or title to the Eastern territories.[170]

Another wrinkle in the argument favoring the validity of the Gorlitz Agreement is the fact that in 1950 the Four Powers were still technically, and legally, at war with Germany. The state of war, absent a peace treaty, was only ended by unilateral declaration of all four powers in 1955[171]. No peace treaty of any kind can be concluded between nations still at war! A peace treaty is designed to conclude a state of war, and if Gorlitz was a true peace treaty, which no one has seriously argued, then it would have had to end the state of war, but in fact this was done five years later.

A final interesting argument against the legal authority and validity of East Germany to conclude the Gorlitz Agreement is expressed by Meyer-Lindenberg:

> the rulers of the Soviet zone...have no right whatever to represent the whole of Germany...the Soviet zone, which is not a subject of international law, can for this reason alone not be a partner to agreements in international law...even if, argumenti causa, the Soviet zone were to be accorded subjectivity in international law and thus the ability to conclude a treaty, the Government of the Zone would not be entitled to cede the eastern German territories, if only for the reason that the areas beyond the Oder-Neisse-Line have never been under the jurisdiction of the Pankow authorities.[172]

If we follow the Soviet argument that Potsdam seperated the Oder-Neisse Territories from the rest of Germany and placed them under the

"administration" of Poland and the Soviet Union, then they were long removed before the D.D.R. had even been created. Under the Soviet interpretation of Potsdam, the Gorlitz Agreement is a useless scrap of paper with no meaning or validity under law, as it seems to give away what the Poles claim was already given. Is this the true interpretation of Gorlitz, or does the Agreement in fact indicate that even the Poles realised that Potsdam gave away nothing? If the latter interpretation is valid, the effects are far-reaching. The creation of the D.D.R. clearly violated the intentions of at least three of the Four Powers occupying Germany and responsible for her fate. Its legal status, at least in 1950, prior to recognition by all but one of the Allied states, was tenuous at best, and the treaties that the D.D.R. entered into may very well be found invalid. If so, any territorial change through the Gorlitz Agreement would be invalid. On the other hand, the action of Gorlitz indicates that no one seriously challenges the provisional status of Potsdam. Therefore, no legally binding agreement exists that changes the sovereignty over the Oder-Neisse Territories from what it was in 1938.

There are also many arguments on the side that supports the valid status under international law of East Germany, and that state's ability to enter into binding international agreements. The basic premise of this school of thought is twofold. First, the Oder-Neisse frontier was settled at the Potsdam Conference, and that decision is the legal justification for the new frontier[173]. Second, in 1945 the old German Reich ceased to exist, and has never since existed, being replaced by two equal and separate states, neither of which can claim to be successors of the Reich[174]. While East Germany recognized West Germany as a sovereign state from its inception, West Germany refused to do the same until much later, and even today this "recognition" is very conditional.

The issue of the legal validity of the Potsdam Agreement has been dealt with above, and need not be detailed again here. The important point to note is that if Potsdam is the instrument that gave legal title of the Oder-Neisse Territories to Poland, the Gorlitz Agreement can be nothing more than a technical frontier regime treaty. In fact the name of the treaty would indicate this from the wording in the title "...Demarcation of **the Established and Existing** Polish-German State Frontier" (emphasis added). The parties were merely confirming and delimiting in detail the political decision already made by the Three Powers[175]. An argument closely related to this point is that German territory could be taken from Germany by the Allied Powers in 1945, as the German state had ceased to exist and the only government, the Allied Control Commission (which had become due to Germany's sovereign disappearance the sovereign of Germany), could take the actions allowed of a sovereign state[176]. In effect,

the Allies could do whatever they wished with Germany in 1945, as they were legally in control of that state. This argument seems to be the sophisticated version of "to the victors belong the spoils", which was certainly true in state practice up to that time, but its compatability with the U.N. Charter is open to question.

The issue of whether the German state ceased to exist in 1945 is crucial in that this one point will decide a number of other issues relating to the frontiers. First, if Germany did cease to exist in 1945 then the Allies may well have obtained absolute control over Germany, and could dictate any terms or give and take territory at will, as if it were their own. No German states emerged to take the place of the German state defunct in 1945 until 1949, and in this interim period the Potsdam Declaration was signed by the only authorities controlling Germany[177]. Indeed many writers hail the dissolution of Prussia, symbol to some of militarism and the threatening German "Drang nach Osten", as having occurred in 1945 [178]. If indeed Prussia, a state within the German nation, ceased to exist in 1945 then this would indicate that the whole nation may have ceased to exist. A great portion of Prussia was theoretically lost to Poland when the Oder-Neisse Territories were occupied, and one of the first acts of East Germany in 1949 was to reorganize the administrative districts in its territory and officially abolish the state of Prussia. Likewise in the west there is no rump state of Prussia (very little Prussian territory actually lay in what is now West Germany anyway). Furthermore, there was no German government after the Flensberg officers were arrested by the Allies in mid-May, 1945, and even areas of Germany still in the control of the German army were, after the surrender, taken over by the occupation authorities. This contrasts with the Germany of 1919. Local German administrators remained at their posts out of necessity, but no central German government existed in any area until possibly the "Bizonia" situation created in 1948. Since May, 1945 no central government has run Germany, unless one considered the Allied Control Commission situated in Berlin as a "central" government. However, this body was firstly not German, and secondly it never was able to agree on any central policies that worked. In the end each occupation power governed its zone as it saw fit, and two "states" were created due to the inability of the Allies to agree on a common policy for a united Germany. If the German state continued to exist unimpeded through all of this, where was it?

One important argument is that the Allies were still technically at war with Germany until 1955. While hostilities ceased in 1945, the legal state of war between the Allies and Germany continued until the various Allied Powers made unilateral declarations of termination of hostilities with Germany in 1954 and 1955 (almost ten years after the Potsdam

Conference), and even then the U.S., Britain and France recognised and made a peace declaration only with West Germany, while the Soviet Union declared an end of hostilities only with East Germany[179]. In 1955 the Soviet Union signed a treaty of recognition with West Germany, the first European power to recognize both German entities[180]. Polish writers argue that the fact that the Soviet Union recognizes both German States legally ends any state of war existing between Germany and Russia, and thus the provisions of the Potsdam Agreement (which some scholars argued that as a peace agreement could not be applied while Germany was in a legal state of war) could now be applied[181]. On the contrary, other Polish writers seem to believe that the Soviet recognition of both German States in 1955 had no bearing upon the validity of the Potsdam Agreement or the Oder-Neisse Territories. Wiewiora uses the example of the Gorlitz Agreement between Poland and East Germany in 1950 to show that frontier changes could be made even when a technical state of war still existed between states[182]. In fact, Wiewiora goes on to argue that because both German States entered into numerous economic, military and other treaties with various states, including former enemies, and joined various international organizations, the liquidation of the legal state of war had taken place without the signing of a treaty of peace, although this termination of hostilities was confined to the western Allies in the case of West Germany[183]. We noted above that the lack of the Western Powers' recognition of the Oder-Neisse Frontier and the D.D.R. is considered by Polish and Russian proponents to be of no effect under international law. At least one Polish author, while not arguing the legal necessity of recognition, gives examples of numerous states' recognition of the two new German States as proof of both the legal existance of the D.D.R. and the frontier settlement[184]. The very reliance by Polish protagonists on multinational recognition of the German state(s) as a prerequisite to a territorial settlement indicates that the German Reich had to continue to exist in some form. One scholar gives strong support for the idea that "Germany" as a nation continued to exist undivided after the War. He writes:

> Thus after the defeat of Nazi Germany in the Second World War the four major Allied powers assumed supreme power in Germany. The legal competence of the German state did not, however, disappear. What occurred is akin to legal representation or agency of necessity. The German state continued to exist, and, indeed, the legal basis of the occupation depended on its continued existence.[185]

As a consequence, so did the state of war until 1955, nullifying any "treaties" signed with "Germany" before that time.

Several scholars in both Poland and West Germany indicate that the reunification of Germany and the conclusion of a peace treaty with a united "all-German government" would not affect the legal status of the Oder-Neisse Line. The argument goes back predictably to the old saw that Potsdam was the final legal settlement of the frontier. Applied to this situation, this means that reunification would have no bearing since even the treaties concluded by the two separate German States, such as Gorlitz, have not created the Oder-Neisse Line, which was already in existance by the actions of the Great Powers, over which Germany, after surrender in 1945, had no control[186]. Other writers argue that the situation of the two Germanies after 1950 was at least de facto settled, and therefore any reunification could only be undertaken if West Germany would recognize East Germany within its present frontiers, as Russia and Poland did for West Germany[187].

This begs the question of what is meant by the term "reunification". To West Germany this would entail, at least before 1970, the formation of an all-German government within the frontiers of 1937, while for other states, including the West, this meant, according to some authorities, only the unification of the B.R.D. and D.D.R.[188]. Thus even if a peace treaty with a united Germany was legally necessary to confirm the frontier changes, and this is denied by most pro-Polish sources, it might be very difficult to determine when the appropriate situation had been reached to allow the peace treaty to be negotiated, as it is unclear in scholastic and diplomatic circles exactly how much of pre-1945 Germany must be unified to become the "unified all-German government". The importance of the legal status of the German State or States for the Oder-Neisse controversy is no better clarified than when we review the legal problem of cession of territory. As Whiteman succinctly puts it, "International law prescribes no particular form in which cession of territory must take place. All that matters is that the cession takes place with the full consent of the Governments concerned"[189]. The most problematic question is therefore whether any valid German government that is entitled to speak for the Oder-Neisse Territories has ever "consented" to their cession to Poland. From the discussion above, the only possible answer to this query is a firm "no".

One last issue as to the legal status of the Oder-Neisse Territories prior to the treaties of 1970 is the effect of prescriptive claims, both by Germany as a result of occupation up to 1945, and by Poland since 1945. The concept of prescription has been recognized since the time of Grotius as a valid method of obtaining title to territory under international law. This method involves the taking by conquest or otherwise of territory belonging to another state and holding this territory for a period of time without protest or other action from the former occupant that would indicate that

the former state still raises claims to the territory. German scholars acknowledge that prescription "applies even if the original seizure was obviously legally invalid, but the state suffering injury raises no claims and the community of nations does not consider that there are grounds for interference"[190]. The exact time that is required to obtain legal title may still be open to debate. Meyer-Lindenberg quotes Oppenheim as stating that the time required should be as much "as is necessary to create under the influence of historical development the general conviction that the present condition of things is in conformity with international order"[191]. Grotius considered that 100 years was a minimum time for a prescriptive title to become valid[192]. In some later treaties the period of time was found to be shorter, as in the case of the Treaty of 1897 between Great Britain and Venezuela concerning the boundary of British Guiana, where fifty years was declared sufficient for a prescriptive claim to become good. Indeed in modern times the waiting period may have become shorter due to better ability to obtain notice of a prescriptive claim and the lack of any territory (except Antarctica) that is not claimed by some state. The International Court of Justice addressed a boundary dispute between Cambodia and Thailand where a boundary survey mistakenly drawn had been accepted by both parties. The Court held that after fifty years the boundary line prescribed, even where one party did not realize some of the implications, *as long as* the line was agreed upon by both parties willingly and freely[193]. As Whiteman has noted:

> Since the advent of the Covenant of the League of Nations, the Pact of Paris and the Charter of the United Nations, treaty-making under duress has been rendered illegal...Consequently, the only means open to the conqueror to make good his title is through the process of prescription, unless "debellatio" has taken place and been followed by annexation or the creation of a new subject of international law.[194]

Whiteman does not specify what period of time is required for a prescriptive claim to take hold, but only states that it must be "a considerable length of time"[195]. This must mean at least fifty years, although that term is found in only one treaty. Even if we take the longer Grotian figure of 100 years, adopted by the Permanent Court of International Justice as a standard in 1933, we will find interesting results with respect to the German and Polish claims to the Oder-Neisse Territories[196].

As we have seen from the historical survey above, whether German or Polish accounts are taken, German title to the Oder-Neisse Territories

was firmly established at the latest around 1400 A.D. East Prussia, except for the Ermland, was never occupied by either Poland or Russia before 1945, and Poland's only connection with that province was the fiefdom relationship between 1466 and 1648. Even then East Prussia was ruled by German dukes and populated by Germans. Pomerania was under continuous German rule from the Thirteenth Century, and Silesia from about the same time, or by Polish accounts from the early Fifteenth Century. East Brandenberg was German from the Twelfth Century or before. In fact, if we address the strictly Polish prescriptive claims to these areas, barring other Slavic occupations, the era of Polish occupation of these territories (if any), is constricted to at most a time period from roughly 600 A.D. to 1200A.D., a maximum of 600 years in a history that extends back over 3000 years. The Germans at least held these territories from 1300 to 1945, a period of 645 years, in addition to an original occupation of many centuries before the Slavic invasions of the Seventh Century. Not only is the period of most recent German rule longer than the entire era of Polish domination of the Territories, and certainly more recent (covering the time when the theory of prescription in modern relations between states was recognized), but the Poles were not the original claimants to the land. Of course the Russians never did have any claims. Most important of all, there is no indication that Poland actively made claims towards Silesia, Pomerania or East Prussia at any time between 1300 A.D. and at least the post-World War One era, never interrupting the prescriptive process of 600 or more years. Poland existed as a state until 1795, and again beginning in 1919. In the earlier period no claims were made to the German lands, and in 1919 only extremists called for annexation of the Oder-Neisse Territories. The Polish Government, the only legal body capable of making claims to interrupt a prescriptive process, was satisfied with Posen and West Prussia (although the latter also may have been validly annexed by Prussia by prescription). By 1919 prescription, even under the longer Grotian formula, had certainly taken hold in the Territories. Thus Poland held no legal claim to the Territories in 1919, much less in 1945, based on any invalid German claim.

The Polish claims since 1945 seem weak, and significantly Polish protagonists do not address the prescription argument with any force, as the historical facts would not support their claims. A Russian scholar argues that the German prescriptive claims are likewise invalid. He states:

> The arguments of the West German jurists, who claim the prescriptive right of German possession with respect to the western Slovak lands, are also groundless. Prescription serves as a "legislation" by time of former conquest, as a means of "juridical" justification for annexations of

populated territories... The historical rights are based on the principle of the self-determination of peoples.[197]

Yanovsky goes on to argue that prescriptive claims tied in to the self-determination of peoples are invalid when the national composition of the population has been artificially altered by the government, referring no doubt to the Prussian efforts at Germanizing the Poles in the Nineteenth Century. There are many problems with this argument. Ignoring the fact that this writer's argument better supports the German claims against the Polish annexation after 1945, the writer confuses the Germanization efforts that went on in West Prussia and Posen with the Oder-Neisse Territories, where such methods were never employed (in modern times), a mistake willingly made by Polish protagonists to try to prove the Polish nature of all German lands east of the Oder-Neisse. Second, the idea of "self-determination of peoples" is a concept first appearing only after World War One, and was unheared of before the Twentieth Century. If we are to apply a Twentieth Century concept to a legal title that was obtained in the Fifteenth Century, then most of the territorial claims in Europe will have to be reconsidered.

Yanovsky's argument brings up one other consideration, the ethnic composition of the Oder-Neisse Territories and the effect under international law. The argument that these territories were predominantly Polish, or were Germanized only in the Nineteenth Century, is easily refuted. First, historical records from as far back as the Sixteenth Century indicate that Silesia, Pomerania and East Prussia were inhabited predominantly, if not exclusively, by Germans. If that is not enough, Twentieth Century data are more convincing. Woodrow Wilson's Fourteen Points and the Treaty of Versailles called for self-determination of peoples, and the Charters of both the League of Nations and the United Nations embodied this principle, making signatories bound by it. As most of the nations of the World were signatories to both charters and to Versailles, this concept must be considered as having been accepted as a norm of international law (jus cogens) at the latest by 1945. Following both Yanovsky's thesis and principles of jus cogens, we must look to the wishes of the population of the Oder-Neisse Territories. It must be assumed that during the Nazi era in Germany those territories with non-German populations were ruthlessly Germanized, so that by the 1940s they were almost exclusively German. If we disregard this last period and review the last "normal" era, that of the Weimar German period of the 1920s, the wishes of the population of the Oder-Neisse Territories becomes dramatically clear. Plebiscites were held in all areas of the Territories that contained any significant Polish minority (see above). This

action by the victorious Allies of 1919 is itself an admission of which part of these territories could conceivably be claimed as Polish, and which were indisputably German. The areas open to question included much of southern East Prussia and Upper Silesia. Still, in the former over 98% of the population favored Germany, and in the latter at least 60% favored Germany (see above). In Upper Silesia the Allies, rather than leave any significant number of Poles in Germany, divided the area to give most of the Poles to Poland, thereby solving the ethnic claims of both Germany and Poland. If the populations of these mixed border regions voted so overwhelmingly for Germany in 1919, and all significant Polish minority areas were handed to Poland, then what claim does Poland have to supposedly Polish areas remaining in Germany twenty-five years later, in 1945? Surely if the populations of Allenstein and Marienburg voted for Germany in 1919, they would have voted for Germany again in 1945, as under Hitler the population could only have become even more German[198]. While Yanovsky claims that the plebiscite would not apply to the Germans of the Oder-Neisse Territories due to his historically and geographically inaccurate logic, western scholars recognize that plebiscites, especially in the Twentieth Century, are the best method of determining a state's sovereignty over its people[199]. A plebiscite was never used for the population of the Oder-Neisse Territories after World War Two. Perhaps the Poles and Russians knew that this could only create an irrebuttable argument against them[200].

If the Poles at this date make any prescriptive claim to the Oder-Neisse Territories as an alternative to the legal improbabilities of the Potsdam Agreement and the Gorlitz Treaty, their claim would be very weak. For boundary prescription to take hold the former claimant must raise no objection to the occupation by the new claimant[201]. West Germany, supported by numerous Western Powers, raised continuous claims to the Territories at least until 1970 [202], and the Western Powers denounced the unilateral Polish/Soviet claims of annexation as invalid[203]. From this it appears that at best only the years from 1970 to 1989 have passed without German claims interrupting the prescription, and 19 years is too short a time for prescription to take hold even under the dubious British-Venezuelan formula. Even if prescription began in 1945, due to the Polish-East German argument that sovereignty was transfered at Potsdam, only 44 years have passed, still not long enough for a valid prescriptive claim[204]. Yet another block to the prescriptive claim arises with the wording of the Potsdam Declaration. This is the specific placement of the Territories under the "administration" of Poland and the Soviet Union. In an earlier dispute between Egypt and Great Britain (later Israel) over claims to the Sinai Peninsula, detailed above, this exact problem was addressed. Great

Britain took the official view that "whether Egypt in fact exercised a peaceful and continuous possession with the intention of acquiring sovereignty (which is not supported historically) does not really concern us because Egypt was only empowered by Turkey to exercise rights of administration"[205]. Modern scholars agree that one of the prerequisites for a prescriptive claim is that the possession of the prescribing state must be exercised "*a titre de souverain*", meaning that a state cannot acquire title to territory by acquisitive prescription if it merely "administers" territory belonging to another state[206]. Thus the institution of "administration" prohibited an Egyptian legal claim to the Sinai in the same era as Poland was trying the same claim, among others, over the Oder-Neisse Territories. If administration does not give any more sovereign claim than that recognized in the Sinai, then Poland's prescriptive claim has never begun.

Notes

1. Elizabeth Wiskemann, *Germany's Eastern Neighbors*, 70 (1956); Friedrich Heiss (ed.), *Deutschland und der Korridor*, 307 (1939). The author has personally heard accounts of several Poles who advocated a frontier on the Elbe. This viewpoint was not as isolated as one would think.

Note: In the chapter dealing with the legal status of the Oder-Neisse Territories from 1945 to 1970 I have attempted to use only works written before 1970, as there is always the problem that any book or article written after 1970, even if addressing the Potsdam era, may be tainted by the Treaties of 1970 and subsequent events. Exceptions to this commitment have been made only when using works dealing with history or general legal theory not specifically addressing the Oder-Neisse Problem.

2. In November, 1939 Wladyslaw Sikorski, the Prime Minister of the exiled Polish Government in London, asked the Governments of Great Britain and France to guarantee Poland more territory after the war, including a "longer seacoast". Friedrich von Wilpert, *The Oder-Neisse Problem*, 55 (1969).

3. In France, the December 22, 1939 issue of *Narodowiec* stated: "after the present war with Germany, Poland must keep, among other things, East Prussia, in order to be able to play the role of haven of freedom between the Baltic and Black Sea." Wilpert, *Supra*, at 55. A more extreme Polish territorial nationalism was expressed in the May, 1940 issue of *Polska Walczaca*: "The boundaries of Polish living space are: in the north the Baltic, in the west the Oder river, in the southwest the Sudetenland, in the south the Moravian Gap and the Carpathian mountains, in the southeast the Dnieper and finally in the northeast the Dvina." Wilpert, *Supra*, at 56.

4. Whiteman, "German-Polish Frontier", 3 *Digest of International Law* 283, 284 (1963); Wilpert, *Supra*, at 54.

5. Wiskemann, *Supra*, at 113.

6. John Blum, *Woodrow Wilson and the Politics of Morality*, P.145ff. (1956). This annexation was embodied in the Treaty of Versailles, which gave West Prussia and Posen to Poland and formed the "Polish Corridor" between Pomerania and East Prussia. Karl von Loesch, "Wie die Ostgebiete des Reiches verlorengingen" *Deutschland und der Korridor* (Friedrich Heiss, ed.), 113 (1939).

7. *Treaty of Versailles*, June 28, 1919. 225 C.T.S. 189. Article 27. Blum, *Supra*, at 147ff. Even in the case of Germany in 1919, the cession of other territories, such as northern Schleswig and eastern Upper Silesia, were ordered only after plebiscites determined that the majority of their respective populations wished to join the neighboring state. In the case of the territorial breakup of the Austro-Hungarian Empire most of the ethnic areas had already declared their independence before the conclusion of hostilities, making their "self-determination" a *fait accompli*, while in the case of the Ottoman Empire representatives of the Arab minorities actually attended the Versailles conference to lobby for their independence.

8. 397 H.C. Deb. (5th Ser.) col. 698 (Feb. 22, 1944).

9. 397 H.C. Deb. (No.35) 936-37 (May 24, 1944).

10. Boleslaw Wiewiora, "West German Territorial Claims Against Poland and International Law", 2 *Polish Western Affairs* 3, 9-11 (1961). This article was first published in Polish as: Boleslaw Wiewiora, "Zachodnioniemieckie roszczenia terytorialne wobec Polski a prawo miedzynarodowe", 15 *Panstwo i Prawo* 923 (Dec., 1960). See also: Richard Staar, "The Polish-German Boundary: A Case Study in International Law", 11 *Journal of Public Law* 155, 157 (1962). Staar mentions Churchill's statement, but also argues that the Teheran Conference communique of 1943 remained consistent with the Atlantic Charter by mentioning no territorial changes.

11. Boleslaw Wiewiora, *Polish-German Frontier from the Standpoint of International Law*, 4 (1959); Wiskemann, *Supra* at 66.

12. Wiewiora, *Polish-German Frontier* at 3.

13. 59 Stat. 1031, T.S. No.993.

14. Cordell Hull, *The Memoirs of Cordell Hull* (Vol.II), 1712 (1948).

15. Jurists in the Soviet Union have in any case indicated that they adhere to the concept of no territorial aggrandizement as a valid principle of international law. See: S.V. Molodtsov, "Peaceful Settlement of Territorial Disputes and Frontier Issues" (summary in English), 1962 *Sovetstii Ezhegodnik Mezhdunarodnogo Prava* 70, 81.

16. This however would be a glaring violation of international law as recognized in the post-1945 period. The prohibition of territorial annexation by means of war has become a principle of jus cogens. In the Vienna Convention on the Law of Treaties, Article 53 prohibits treaties in conflict with any principle of jus cogens. *Vienna Convention on the Law of Treaties*, May 22, 1969. 8 I.L.M. 679.

17. *Vienna Convention on the Law of Treaties*, U.N. Doc. A/CONF. 39/27, at 289 (1969), 8 I.L.M. 679 (1969). Article 53 states that treaties conflicting with a peremptory norm of general international law (*jus cogens*) are void.

18. For examples of conventions and treaties denouncing cession by conquest before World War Two see: Whiteman, "Cession", *Supra*, P.1115-1118. For abrogation of Brest-Litovsk see: *Treaty of Versailles*, *Supra*, Article 116.

19. Whiteman, "Cession", *Supra*, at 1114.

20. Alfred de Zayas, *Nemisis at Potsdam*, 42 (1977).

21. Wiskemann, *Supra* at 74.

22. Hull, *Supra*, Vol. II, at 1316.

23. *Id*.

24. Churchill, *Closing the Ring*, 403 (1951). Churchill went on to write that "The Curzon Line, subject to interpretation in the East, and the line of the Oder in the West, seemed to afford a true and lasting home for the Polish nation after all its suffering." *Id*. at 406.

25. Tony Sharp, "The Russian Annexation of the Königsberg Area, 1941-45", 23 *Survey* 156 (1977-78). Before Teheran the United States had favored giving all of East Prussia to Poland, as was apparent from discussions between Roosevelt and Mikolajczyk, Sikorski's successor as head of the Polish government in exile in London, and later between Roosevelt and Eden. See; de Zayas, *Supra* at 40.

26. Churchill, *Supra*, P.403.

27. Sarah Terry, *Poland's Place in Europe*, 348 (1983).

28. Holborn (ed.), *War and Peace Aims of the United Nations*, 12 (1948).

29. Terry, *Supra*, at 347. A crucial issue related to the Königsberg territory, but one which neither the Big Three or future writers ever addressed, was the Russian annexation of Estonia, Latvia and Lithuania. The territory of Lithuania separated northern East Prussia, including Königsberg, from the Soviet Union. In 1940 Russian troops moved into the Baltic States and after holding rigged "elections" announced that these three nations had opted to become part of the Soviet Union, a situation not recognized by the Western Powers during or after the War. However, unless the Königsberg territory was going to become for Russia what it had been for Germany between 1919 and 1939, a territory separated from the mother country by the intervening territory of another state, then Western acquiescence in the Russian annexation would seem to indicate acceptance of the Russian subjugation of Lithuania, in clear violation of the Atlantic Charter and subsequent United Nations policies.

30. The Polish-Soviet border was established by the Treaty of Riga on March 18, 1921, and confirmed in a non-aggression pact signed on July 25, 1932, which specifically guaranteed the borders set by the Treaty of Riga. Woolsey, "The Polish Boundary Question", 38 *The American Journal of International Law* 441, 443 (1944).

31. This was due to a number of reasons. First and foremost was of course the unspoken dispute over the eastern frontier of Poland, for the Poles had been vocal in their demand for the pre-1939 eastern frontier, while the Russians never renounced the 1939 annexation. Relations worsened in 1942 when hundreds of Polish army officers were found murdered in the Katyn Forest. International experts called in by the Germans determined, and even the Russians could not refute the evidence, that these Poles had been killed shortly after the Russians occupied eastern Poland in 1939. This was part of the Russian plan to subjugate Poland as the Germans tried to do in western Poland. Terry, *Supra*, 247-250.

32. The notable exception was the dispute over the city of Lwow, located east of the Curzon Line but ethnically Polish. The London Poles adamantly refused to give up Lwow, and the British stood behind them. It is probably because of the dispute over Lwow that a definite agreement about the Polish-Soviet frontier was not reached at Teheran.

Wartime alliances faced with a strong enemy such as Germany often make states agree, in the interest of ending the current threat, to compromises that in other times would be abhorrent to them. How else could one explain the ease with which the Russians managed to get the Western Allies to accept their claim to eastern Poland, which they had conquored in 1939 in alliance with Nazi Germany, in violation of their non-aggression pact with Poland, and despite the fact that in 1929 Russia had joined Poland, Estonia, Latvia and Romania in signing a Protocol in Moscow that brought them into the Pact of Paris of August 27, 1928 renouncing war as an instrument of national policy? See: Woolsey, *Supra* at 444.

33. Zoltan Szaz, *Germany's Eastern Frontiers*, 81 (1960).

34. Z. Anthony Kruszewski, *The Oder-Neisse Boundary and Poland's Modernization*, 12 (1972).

35. Staar, *supra* at 158. For the argument that the Western Allies supported a Polish frontier as far west as the Oder out of a sense of guilt at giving away eastern Poland, see: de Zayas, *Supra*, P.41.

36. *Id.*

37. Wiskemann, *Supra* at 74-76.

38. W. Drzewieniecki, *The German-Polish Frontier*, 56 (1959); Z. Jordan, *Oder-Neisse Line*, 7-9 (1952); de Zayas, *Supra* at 44; Wiskemann, *Supra* at 75; Terry, *Supra* at 347-49. The almost desperate attempts by the Western Powers to bring the London Poles and the Soviets into some sort of agreement is described by Churchill. Stalin apparantly recognized this Western weakness and became firm in his demand for the Curzon Line, with Lwow going to Russia. Churchill, *Supra*, at 395-96.

39. Kruszewski, *Supra*, at 14. The idea of compensating Poland for her economic losses with the rich eastern German lands also had great appeal, but was not as decisive as the Allied acquiescence to Soviet annexation of territory in violation of the Allies' basic principles.

40. For this reason some writers argue that Germany is not bound by this or any subsequent decisions, an argument that will be addressed below. Rhode, *Die Ostgebiete des Deutschen Reiches*, 159 (1956). Many argue that Poland did have a strong moral case for compensation, due to the harsh treatment meated out to her by Germany from 1939 to 1945, as war crimes might except the "criminal" state from some principles of international law. In any case the compensation idea was developed by the Allies, not Poland, and Poland never accepted it as reason for annexation of territory. Staar, *Supra*, at 169, 173.

41. Whiteman, *Supra* at 295. The text of a joint statement issued by British Foreign Minister Eden and U.S. Secretary of State Stettinius issued on February 1st, 1945, just prior to the opening of the Yalta Conference reads: "As regards Poland's western frontier, we... agreed that Poland should certainly have East Prussia, south and west of Königsberg, Danzig, the eastern tip of Pomerania and the whole of Upper Silesia...We were prepared last October in Moscow to let Mr. Mikalajczyk's government have any territories they chose to claim up to the Oder, but this was conditional upon agreement then being reached between him and the Russians, and there was no question of our agreeing to the Western Neisse frontier. I also think that we should keep the position fluid...since we need not make the same concessions to the Lublin Poles which we were prepared to make

to Mr. Mikalajaczyk in order to obtain a solution of the Polish problem." Szaz, *Supra*, P.88.

42. In Silesia there are two Neisse rivers. The Western or Lausatian Neisse flows into the Oder at Frankfurt-on-Oder, and is the southern part of the presently-disputed border. The Eastern Neisse flows into the Oder well east of Breslau, and more or less corresponds to the western border of the Oppeln District, which composes most of the Upper Silesia industrial region and was the area of the 1921 plebiscite, as well as the part of Silesia that the Western powers were willing to give to Poland. As we shall see, the debate over which Neisse river would form the new frontier would be the hottest, and most indefinitely settled, part of the Yalta and Potsdam Conferences.

43. Drzewieniecki, *Supra*, at 59-60.

44. de Zayas, *Supra*, at 53-54; Wiskemann, *Supra*, at 83-85.

45. Edward Stettinius, *Roosevelt and the Russians*, 86 (1949).

46. Winston Churchill, *Triumph and Tragedy*, 374 (1953). Mr. Churchill stated to the other delegates that "it would be a great pity to stuff the Polish goose so full of German food that it died of indigestion". *Id*. Another problem that bothered the western delegates was what would be done with the millions of German nationals that inhabited these territories. This crucial issue will be dealt with in depth below.

47. Stettinius, *Supra*, at 155.

48. Churchill, *Triumph and Tragedy*, *Supra*, at 376-77.

49. *Id*.

50. Stettinius, *Supra*, at 258-60.

This would seem to indicate that when the Western Allies referred to the Polish Provisional Government of National Unity from this time forward, they expected it to be representative of all non-fascist parties, especially the London Poles, and/or that its representatives were freely elected. As the Polish government set up in Lublin and later moved to Warsaw never included any political elements but Moscow-approved Communist Party members, one must question whether the Western Powers would have made the same promises as they were willing to give to a democratic Poland.

51. Holborn, *Supra*, at 24.

52. Wiewiora, *Polish-German Frontier*, *Supra*, at 61.

53. Wright, "Poland and the Crimea Conference",39 *The American Journal of International Law* 300, 306 (1945).

54. Wright, *Supra*, at 307.

55. Wiewiora, *Supra*, at 63-67.

56. *Id*.

57. Wiewiora, *Supra*, P.65.

58. Some writers, mostly Polish, consider that both the Yalta and Potsdam agreements had a "constitutive character" and were therefore legally binding, comparable to the United Nations Charter, inasmuch as the Great Powers were the paramount authorities during the War and apparantly their decisions, even regarding third-party states not present at the Conferences, are valid international law. Wiewiora, *Supra*, at 33-38. However, other scholars do not view the Yalta or, in some cases, the Potsdam decisions as legally binding. See: Briggs, "The Leader's Agreement - Yalta", 40 *The American Journal of International Law* 376 (1946);

Pan, "Legal Aspects of the Yalta Agreement", 46 *The American Journal of International Law* 40 (1952).

59. The exception is Wiewiora, who argues that even the Yalta Conference set the frontier at the Oder and Western Neisse, based upon discussions during the Conference, not on the final declaration. Wiewiora, *Supra*, at 61-67.

60. Wiewiora, *Supra*, at 94-113.

61. Whiteman, *Supra*, at 298-99.

62. Whiteman, *Supra*, P.300.

63. Kruszewski, *Supra*, at 26-27.

64. Whiteman, *Supra*, at 300-302; Sassa, "The Prelude to the Expulsions and Oder-Neisse Line from 1939-1945",2 *Eastern Germany* 412 (1963).

65. Whiteman, *Supra*, at 303.

66. *Id*.

67. Whiteman, *Supra*, P.304-07. While the Americans were operating under the assumption that the Four Power Berlin Declaration was in effect, Marshall Zhukov, the commander of the Soviet occupation forces, declared that the Yalta Declaration had established the Polish frontier on the Oder-Neisse, and refused to ship Silesian coal to western Germany!

68. Staar, *Supra*, at 160.

69. Rep. Reece, "On German Provinces East of the Oder-Neisse Line, and Economic, Historical, Legal and Political Aspects Involved", 103 *Congressional Record* 7117, 7118 (1957).

70. Reece, *Supra*, at 7119.

71. For arguments that it is a legally binding agreement on all states, see: Subbarao, "Polish Case for the Oder-Neisse Frontier: A Juridical View",9 *The Indian Journal of International Law* 78 (1969); Wiewiora, *Supra*, at 68-93. For an interesting argument from a pro-Polish source that the Potsdam Declaration only created a de facto situation, and thus by implication was not a legal instrument that could create a de jure transfer of territory, see: Drzewieniecki, *Supra*, at 64-72. A German writer that denies the legal validity of Potsdam has put out two works. See: Kraus, *Die Oder-Neisse Linie* (1954) and Kraus, *The Status Under International Law of the Eastern Territories of Germany Within the Frontiers of the Reich as at 31st December, 1937* (1963). For a German source that recognizes the legality of the Potsdam Declaration (although he argues that it does not make any changes in the German frontiers) see: Rhode, *Supra*, at 160-63.

72. This was conducted in the famous railroad car in the Argonne Forest in France, which was used 21 years later by Hitler for the military surrender of France.

73. Watt, *The Kings Depart*, at 414-486 (1968).

74. *Case Concerning Certain German Interests in Polish Upper Silesia* (Germany v. Poland). 1926 P.C.I.J., ser. A, No.7, at 25-34 (Judgment of May 25th).

75. The implications of the Upper Silesia opinion will be dealt with in more detail below, especially with regard to the rights of the German inhabitants of the Oder-Neisse Territories.

76. Whiteman, *Supra*, at 306-09. The specific wording of the briefing book includes the following: "There is no historic or ethnic justification for the cession of this area (as well as of the trans-Oder region referred to immediately above) to Poland. Such action would doubtless create economic and population difficulties

of the greatest magnitude for Germany and arouse an intense spirit of irredentism. Maintenance of the Oder-Neisse frontier might well become the most critical security problem in Europe during the coming years."

77. Churchill, *Triumph and Tragedy*, *Supra*, at 648.

78. *Id.*; Churchill, *Closing the Ring*, *Supra*, at 406. Apparantly British popular opinion was no more in favor of giving large parts of Germany to Poland, especially if that country's government was now Soviet-dominated. In mid-July the British ambassador in Washington informed the U.S. State Department that "His Majesty's Government have always doubted whether British public opinion would lastingly support a settlement involving the amputation of about one-fifth of the total area of Germany normally inhabited by over ten million persons of undisputably German stock..." Whiteman, *Supra*, at 312.

79. Whiteman, *Supra*, at 309.

80. Charles Mee, *Meeting at Potsdam*, 175-78 (1975).

81. *Id*.

82. Mee, *Supra*, at 180.

83. *Id*.

84. Whiteman, *Supra*, at 316.

85. *Id*.

86. Whiteman, *Supra*, at 316.

87. Whiteman, *Supra*, at 318.

88. Whiteman, *Supra*, at 328. See discussion of the Lithuanian problem above and below.

89. See: Drzewieniecki, *Supra*, at 68; Wiewiora, *Supra*, at 92; Subbarao, *Supra*, at 85.

90. Churchill, *Triumph and Tragedy*, *Supra*, at 648.

91. Mee, *Supra*, at 229.

92. Churchill, *Closing the Ring*, *Supra*, at 406.

93. Feis, *Between War and Peace*, 262 (1960).

94. Stettinius, *Supra*, at 261.

95. Sharp, *Supra*, at 159-60.

96. Mee, *Supra*, at 328. The entire Potsdam Declaration is reproduced in full in: Mee, *Supra*, at 316-335.

97. Kruszewski, *Supra*, at 24.

98. Sharp, *Supra*, at 161.

99. However, some statesmen at the time thought the Russian claim for an ice-free port at Königsberg factually groundless, as Königsberg was actually not ice-free in mid-winter, and furthermore it lay up a long canal and was inaccessible to many vessels year round. Besides, the Russians already had a much better port that was totally ice-free all year, that of Hango on the Finnish coast. Others named Libau, Windau and other ports in the Baltic States as alternative ports for the Russians. See: Sharp, *Supra*.

100. For a good account of the Russian occupation of Lithuania see: Jurgela, *Lithuania: The Outpost of Freedom*, (1974).

101. This situation might have caused the Russians to renounce any claims to Königsberg, as their only important use for the area was as a forward naval base. See: Peitsch, *Wir Kommen aus Königsberg: Nordostpreussen Heute*, (1979). In fact, the United States refused to recognize the incorporation of the Baltic States into

the Soviet Union after World War Two, and continued to refuse recognition even after the 1970 treaties. See: Fifield, "The Postwar World Map: New States and Boundary Changes", 42 *The American Political Science Review* 530, 536 (1948). Consulates for all three republics are maintained to this day in Washington and London. Some argument can be made that when the U.S. signed the Helsinki Accords in 1975 she recognized the incorporation of Lithuania as part of the "present frontiers" (see below). However, the legal effect of Helsinki is disputed, and as this is the only international instrument that gives any indication of U.S. acquiescence in the annexation, the question may still be open. Unfortunately, the issue of the Baltic States is too voluminous to be dealt with hear, but may be even more of an open issue in 1987 than the Oder-Neisse Line.

An interesting if purely technical question relating to northern East Prussia is the status of the Memelland. This territory might have "fallen through the cracks" of the Potsdam Agreement. As we have seen, the Memelland became an autonomous trusteeship of Lithuania in 1924, and was never an integral part of Lithuania, having continuous ties to the League of Nations. See: *Interpretation of the Statute of the Memel Territory*, P.C.I.J. Ser. A./B, No.49 (1932). It was legally returned to Germany by treaty in 1939 (see above) but was not included in the Königsberg territory to be assigned to Russia after 1945. At the same time no international agreement has nullified the valid German-Lithuanian Treaty of 1939, nor for that matter the League of Nations trusteeship of 1924. As long as Lithuania and Königsberg remain under Soviet domination this great oversight will have no effect on boundaries. If, however, either territory is found to be illegally held by the Soviet Union, possession of Memel will become a crucial matter.

102. Sharp, *Supra*, at 162.

103. Mee, *Supra*, at 330.

104. Mee, *Supra*, at 330-31. For another complete text of the Potsdam Declaration, see: Holborn, *Supra*, at 40-53.

105. Wiewiora, *Supra*, at 94 ff.

106. See for example: Klafkowski, "The forms of Recognition of State Frontiers after the Second World War", *Jahrbuch fur Ostrecht*, 71, 79 (1964); Wiewiora, "West German Territorial Claims Against Poland and International Law", 2 *Polish Western Affairs*, 3, 20-21 (1961); Subbarao, *Supra*, at 85.

107. Meyer-Lindenberg, "Deutschlands Grenzen: Die Aussage des Volkerrechts", *Internationales Recht und Diplomatie*, (1961).

108. P.K. Menon, "International Boundaries - A Case Study of the Guyana-Surinam Boundary", 27 *International and Comparative Law Quarterly* 738, 742 (Oct., 1978).

109. *Case Concerning Sovereignty over Certain Frontier Land* (Belgium v. Netherlands). (1959) I.C.J. 209.

110. *Id*.

111. See: deZayas, *Supra*, at 158-59.

112. *Treaty between Austria-Hungary, France, Germany, Great Britain, Italy, Russia and Turkey for the Settlement of Affairs in the East* (Berlin Treaty), 13 July, 1878. 153 C.T.S. 171.

The actual wording of the Article reads as follows: "Les Provinces de Bosnie et d'Herzegovine seront occupees et administrees par l'Autriche-Hongrie.

Le Gouvernement d'Autriche-Hongrie ne desirant pas se charger de l'administration du Sandjak de Novi-Bazar, qui s'etend entre la Serbie et le Montenegro dans la direction sud-est jusqu'au dela de Mitrovitza, l'Administration Ottomane continuera d'y fonctionner. Neanmoins, afin d'assurer le maintien du nouvel etat politique ainsi que la liberte et la securite des voies de comminication, l'autriche-Hongrie se reserve le droit de tenir garnison et d'avoir des routes militaires et commerciales sur toute l'etendue de cette partie de l'ancien Vilayet de Bosnie. A cet effet les Gouvernements d'Autriche-Hongrie et de Turquie se reservent de s'entendre sur les details."

113. Whiteman, "Cession", at 1105.

114. 484 H.C. Deb., Col. 1271 (Feb. 20, 1951).

115. Munch, "Die Rechtsstellung der Deutschen Ostgebiete", *Internationales Recht und Diplomatie* 29, 35 (1970).

116. Takashi Oka, "Warming Trend Sets in for Soviet-Japanese Ties", *Christian Science Monitor*, 9 (October 25, 1988).

117. *Lighthouses in Crete and Samos*. P.C.I.J., ser. A/B, no.71 (1937). In fact no persons of Turkish nationality even lived on the islands, and certainly no Turkish officials resided there, since before 1913. Turkey's claim to the islands was certainly more attenuated than Germany's is to the Oder-Neisse Territories, yet the Court's decision is clear.

118. Ian Brownlie, *Principles of Public International Law*, 114-115 (1979).

119. Subbarao, *Supra*, at 84.

120. Jordan, *Supra*, at 12.

121. It is interesting to note that the two Western states at Potsdam were both common-law nations, thus having very similar ideas of legal rights, as domestic law would inevitably influence all but the greatest international legal scholars.

122. Meyer-Lindenberg, *Supra*, at 26.

123. Yanovsky, "The German Peace Treaty and the Oder-Neisse Border", *Sovetstii Ezhegodnik Mezhdunarodnoco*, 150-57, 156 (1962).

124. Staar, *Supra*, at 163.

125. Rosenthal, *German and Pole*, 129-30 (1976). The integration issue makes for interesting discussion when compared with the current situation in Israel/Palestine. While the German expellees were assimilated into western Germany quickly, and given every assistance by the German government to find housing, permanent employment, etc., the refugees from the West Bank and other areas occupied by Israel in 1956 and 1968 have still not been assimilated by neighboring Arab states, but remain in temporary refugee camps with minimal governmental assistance, despite much lip service from Arab nations over the "plight of the Palestinians". Some authorities have speculated that the Arab governments have taken this action to reinforce their non-recognition of the Israeli occupation or annexation of Arab lands, or of the State of Israel itself. If this is true, then the West German government may have made a major blunder in accepting the refugees so easily, contradicting its oft-claimed non-recognition of the situation across the Oder-Neisse.

126. Some writers argue that based on discussions at Potsdam, in which Churchill opposed the transfers as they would cause millions of Germans to flee to the west, the Allies meant to expel the massive number of Germans in the Oder-Neisse Territories, not just the 800,000 or so Germans in Poland proper. In the

confusion reigning in 1945-46, the Western Allies would have no way to determine if the refugees arriving in the west were all from central Poland, or if the Poles and Russians were expelling all of the Germans from eastern Germany.

127. Kraus, *The Status under International Law of the Eastern Territories of Germany within the Frontiers of the Reich as at 31st December, 1937*, (1963).

128. Kraus, *Die Oder-Neisse Linie, Supra*.

129. Subbarao, *Supra*, at 81.

130. Staar, *Supra*, at 161.

131. Staar, *Supra*, at 170. Staar uses the example of Alsace-Lorraine, which was supposedly ceded by Germany back to France on November 11, 1918, the day an armistice was signed, and not in 1919 after the Treaty of Versailles, which made provision for such transfer, had been signed by all parties. The author has not been able to confirm from any sources that this was indeed the fate of Alsace-Lorraine.

132. Watt, *Supra*, at 414-78. Staar, *Supra* at 170 disagrees that Alsace-Lorraine was only ceded at Versailles. See above.

133. Watt, *Supra*, at 478-486.

134. *Certain German Interests in Polish Upper Silesia* (Germany v. Poland). 1926 P.C.I.J., Ser.A, No.7, at 19-31 (Judgment of May 25th).

135. Staar, *Supra*, at 170.

136. Klafkowski, *Supra*, at 73. Interestingly, at least one Russian writer denies that territory can be ceded by one state to another after a war, even through a peace treaty. See: Molodtsov, "Peaceful Settlement of Territorial Disputes and Frontier Issues", 1963 *Sovetski Ezhegodnik Mezhdunarodnogo Prava* 70, 82.

137. Klafkowski, *Supra*, at 72.

138. Klafkowski, *Supra*, at 73. However, certain exceptions to the conquerors rule have been noted, particularly after World War One for moral or "general interest" grounds.

139. Klafkowski, *Supra*, at 72. Still, Klafkowski admits that "neither in theory nor in practice has international law elaborated any general criteria of recognition or of legality of territorial accessions...there are no norms in international law regulating this problem." Klafkowski, *Supra*, at 74.

140. "What is ours, cannot be transferred into other hands without our doing it". Quoted in: Reece, *Supra*, at 1126.

141. Some scholars believe that recognition is not necessary for valid title to fall to the new occupier. See: Staar, *Supra*, at 155. Staar gives the example of areas that are obtained by prescription, or undisputed occupation for long periods, as with the territory in the Island of Palmas Case, decided by the Permanent Court of International Justice.

142. Whiteman, *Supra*, at 354.

143. Whiteman, *Supra*, at 355.

144. Whiteman, *Supra*, at 357. However, some argue that these retrospective statements are not valid to interpret the meaning of agreements made before. In the case of Potsdam the Western Allies' stands changed as a result of the beginning of the Cold War, and thus their attitudes in 1946 and after could not affect their intentions and decisions in 1945. Jordan, *Supra*, at 18-19.

145. Whiteman, *Supra*, at 352-53.

146. *Treaty Between the Polish Republic and the Union of Soviet Socialist*

Republics Concerning the Polish-Soviet State Frontier, 16 August, 1945, (Poland-Soviet Union), 10 U.N.T.S. 193.

147. *Id*.

148. Munch, *Supra*, at 34.

149. For a full record of the discussions at the Foreign Ministers' Conferences at Moscow and London in April, 1947 see: Whiteman, *Supra*, at 365-76. If anything, the Western Powers attempted to revise the territorial situation by demanding that Pomerania and Silesia west of the Eastern Neisse revert to German occupation, and that a "Saar-like" status be set up in Upper Silesia.

150. *Agreement Between the Government of the Polish Republic and the Government of the Union of Soviet Socialist Republics Concerning the Regime on the Soviet-Polish State Frontier*, 8 July, 1948, (Poland-Soviet Union), 37 U.N.T.S. 25. Some writers claim that the Western Allies intended at the time of Potsdam that the territorial changes allegedly made there would be permanent, and only later, with the Cold War, did they change their minds and, in their desire to combat the expansion of the Socialist eastern states, enunciate retrospective opinions contrary to their intentions at Potsdam. Jordan, *Supra*, at 18-22. However, the same claim can be made against the Soviet Union and Poland with hard evidence in the form of the contradictory 1945 and 1948 Treaties.

151. The domestic actions of Poland and Russia in the Oder-Neisse Territories indicates that they intended the territories to be permanently annexed from the start. By November, 1945 Poland had implemented Polish law throughout the Oder-Neisse Territories "administered" by her, and the Territories were redivided into new administrative districts or attached to old Polish districts in central Poland. The Territories were also absorbed into the central economic planning structure and political and defensive system. See: Kruszewski, *Supra*. The Russians acted in similar fashion, but they also resettled ethnic Russians in their territory (Königsberg) and ousted the native Germans sooner than did the Poles (this will be discussed in detail in the last chapter). More importantly, the Russians moved quickly to rename every city, town, hamlet and object in the territory. On July 4, 1946 Königsberg was renamed Kaliningrad after the Soviet President. Scharloff, *Königsberg-Damals und Heute*, 9 (1982); Peitsch, *Supra*. Soon every town was Russsianized, and today only a handful of names even relate to local flora and fauna, most being Russian or Ukrainian. Peteraitis, "Mazosios Lietuvos Vietovardziu Svetimejimas XX Amziuje", (Brakas, ed.) *Lithuania Minor*, 262-72 (1976).

152. *Agreement Between the Polish Republic and the German Democratic Republic Concerning the Demarcation of the Established and Existing Polish-German State Frontier* (Gorlitz or Zgorzelec Agreement), July 6, 1950, (Poland-German Democratic Republic). 1959 U.N.T.S. 104, 105.

153. *Id*.

154. Zieger, "Das Neue Gesetz uber die Staatsgrenze der DDR", 27 *Recht in Ost und West* 1 (Jan., 1983).

155. *Treaty Concerning Relations Between the Union of Soviet Socialist Republics and the German Deomcratic Republic*, September 20, 1955. 226 U.N.T.S. 208.

156. Schwarz, "Adenauer's Ostpolitik" (Hanreider, ed.) *West German Foreign Policy: 1949-1979*, 127, 133 (1980).

157. Schwarz, *Supra* at 130-32.

158. Schwarz, *Supra* at 140-43.

159. Mann, "Germany's Present Legal Status Revisited", 16 *International and Comparative Law Quarterly* 760, 762-63 (July, 1967). This article is an update of a lecture given by Dr. Mann in 1947, in which he argued more or less the same basic points. See: 33 *Transactions of the Grotius Society* 119 (1947).

160. Mann, *Supra* at 765-67.

161. *Id*. It is very interesting to note Mann's last comment that Germany was governed "by **five** different governmental authorities". While his article has nothing to do with the Oder-Neisse Territories directly, it is apparant from this statement that he believes that the territory administered by Poland is only occupied, for Poland is undoubtedly the fifth "occupying" power along with the U.S., Britain, Russia and France.

162. Meyer-Lindenberg, "Deutschlands Grenzen, Die Aussage des Volkerrechts", *Internationales Recht und Diplomatie*, 19 (1964).

163. Meyer-Lindenberg, *Supra*, at 21. Meyer-Lindenberg claims that this "confirmation" is embodied in Section II (3) of the Potsdam Agreement, which states that a treaty will be concluded with Germany "when a Government adequate for the purpose is established."

164. Mann, *Supra*, at 789.

165. Mann, *Supra*, at 769.

166. *Id*.

167. Whiteman, *Supra*, at 384.

168. Meyer-Lindenberg, *Supra*, at 22.

169. Mann, *Supra*, at 775. However, for the argument, described above, that no recognition by other states is needed for the change in the status of territory, possibly including the independence of part of a state, see: Staar, *Supra*, at 155. See also de Zayas, *Supra*, at 154, who argues that the D.D.R. was neither de facto nor de jure a sovereign state, and had no power to conclude any international agreements, nor did the actual rulers of East Germany, the Soviet Occupation Authority.

170. Mann, *Supra*, at 787.

171. de Zayas, *Supra*, at 154-55. For the validity under international law of the action of concluding hostilities by unilateral declaration, see: Klafkowski, *Supra*, at 73.

In 1952 the three Western Powers concluded a convention with West Germany as a condition of the end of military occupation. This convention reserved to the Three Powers their "rights and responsibilities" relating to "Berlin and Germany as a whole". Evidently some sort of "whole" Germany was still considered to exist. More about this convention will be said in the following chapter. *Convention Between the United Kingdom, the United States, France and the Federal Republic of Germany on Relations Between the Three Powers and the Federal Republic of Germany* (Three Power Convention), May 26, 1952. 331 U.N.T.S. 328. Art. 2.

172. Meyer-Lindenberg, *Supra*, at 23.

173. Wiewiora, *Supra*, at 175ff.

174. Poeggel, "Deutschlands Grenzen-Die Aussage des Volkerrechts",13 *Staat und Recht* 21, 22 (March, 1964). This is an interesting article in that it is a reply to the article by Meyer-Lindenberg entitled "Deutschlands Grenzen-Die Aussage desVolkerrechts", cited numerous times in this paper. It is, surprisingly, one of the

few East German articles to address the Oder-Neisse problem, and counters Meyer-Lindenberg on most major points.

175. For a detailed argument that Potsdam is binding upon both German states, see: Wiewiora, *Supra*, at 175-203.

176. Poeggel, *Supra*, at 27-29.

177. This is in obvious contrast to the situation in 1918, when a defeated but unoccupied Germany continued to have a German government uninterrupted except by resignations and frequent elections. Politics (except for the kaiser, who abdicated) continued as before up through the signing of the Treaty of Versailles. This striking difference with 1945 makes more difficult the argument that the legal status of Germany with respect to peace treaties and annexations was the same in 1945 as in 1918.

178. Jordan, *Supra*, at 107-111; Poeggel, *Supra*.

179. Wiewiora, *Supra*, at 208-09.

180. Berezowski, "Zagadnienie granicy polsko-niemieckiej swietle radzieckiego projektu traktatu pokoju z Niemcami", 14 *Panstwo i Prawo* 735, 739 (1959).

181. Berezowski, *Supra* at 738ff.

182. Wiewiora, *Supra*, at 209.

183. *Id*.

184. Libera, "Prawno-miedzynarodowe uznanie suwerennosci Polski nad Ziemiami Zachodnimi", 18 *Panstwo i Prawo* 3, 13ff. (1963).

185. Brownlie, *Supra*, at 111.

186. Wiewiora, *Supra*, at 212.

187. Dunin-Keplicz, "Poland and the Two Germanys", 3 *Afro-Asian and World Affairs* 44, 47-8.

188. *Id*.

189. Whiteman, "Cession", 2 *Digest of International Law* 1088 (1963). Whiteman cites the Permanent Court of International Justice opinion in *Certain German Interests in Polish Upper Silesia* for this point.

190. Deutsches Volkerrecht Verein, *Worterbuch des Volkerrechts*, Vol. I, 620 (1960).

191. Meyer-Lindenberg, *Supra*, at 28.

192. Grotius, cited in: Meyer-Lidenberg, *Supra*.

193. *Case Concerning the Temple of Preah Vihear* (Cambodia v. Thailand). (1962) I.C.J. 6.

194. Whiteman, "Cession", *Supra*, at 1155.

195. *Id*.

196. The 100 year period is supported by the Permanent Court of International Justice in the case of the *Legal Status of Eastern Greenland* (Norway v. Denmark). 6 P.C.I.J. Ser. A./B., No.53 (1933).

197. Yanovsky, *Supra*, at 157.

198. The Prussian census of 1910 indicated that while West Prussia and especially Posen contained a significant amount, probably a majority, of Poles, East Prussia, Silesia and Pomerania were overwhelmingly German, except in the later plebiscite areas. Gayre, *Teuton and Slav on the Polish Frontier*, 18-19 (1944). If the Prussian census-takers had reason to falsify the results in the (then) interior provinces of Pomerania and Silesia, did they not have more reason to falsify results in the frontier provinces of Posen and West Prussia, although these in fact

appeared rather accurate? Even Allied maps prepared for the Potsdam Conference admitted that most of Silesia and Pomerania were 100% German. See: de Zayas, *Supra*.

199. See: Farley, *Plebiscites and Sovereignty*, 1-10 (1986).

200. This issue will be addressed in more detail in the chapter relating to the expulsions.

201. Kaikobad, "Some Observations on the Doctrine of Continuity and Finality of Boundaries", 54 *British Yearbook of International Law* 119 (1982).

202. A detailed list of official West German Government statements denouncing the Oder-Neisse frontier can be found in Reece, *Supra*, at 7130-31. Among Western states refusing to recognize the Oder-Neisse Line at least until 1970 were the United States, Great Britain, France and, most interestingly, the Vatican. In fact the Holy See refused to reorganize dioceses in the Oder-Neisse Territories or to appoint bishops to replace the six German bishops and archbishops expelled from the Territories, and the six German bishops were listed in the Vatican Yearbook as "prevented from exercising the functions of (their) office".

203. Munch, *Supra*, at 33.

204. This brings us back to the complex argument addressed above relating to the legal status of the B.R.D. and D.D.R., and whether either could lay claim to the Territories after 1945, even in order to give them away by treaty (i.e. Gorlitz).

205. Whiteman, *Supra*, at 1105.

206. Johnson, "Acquisitive Prescription in International Law", 27 *British Yearbook of International Law* 332, 344 (1950).

4

THE LEGAL STATUS OF THE ODER-NEISSE TERRITORIES SINCE THE CONCLUSION OF THE WARSAW AND MOSCOW TREATIES OF 1970

No one can deny that the conclusion by West Germany of the Treaty of Warsaw with Poland and the Treaty of Moscow with the Soviet Union in late 1970 have changed considerably the outlook with respect to the Oder-Neisse Line. All Polish-Soviet proponents consider that these Treaties settled once and for all any remaining legal disputes in favor of Poland and Russia, and many Western scholars agree that even if Potsdam was not the legal grant of sovereignty, the Treaties of 1970 were the finale. Even German proponents must admit that the volume of literature on the Oder-Neisse Problem has dwindled to a trickle in the post-1970 period. This may be out of a loss of interest in the issue, as many more current and solvable problems have taken their place on the world stage. No matter what one's position on the Oder-Neisse Problem, it is undeniable that while the Warsaw Pact remains intact and supported by the Soviet Union the Oder-Neisse Territories will remain under Polish and Russian occupation. Still, if a legal problem remains it should not be ignored merely because of a loss of interest or the inability to find a remedy at present. It is impossible to argue that the Potsdam Agreement made a final determination of the Polish-German boundary, and as Gorlitz was admittedly only a confirmation of the Potsdam Agreement it is no better a legal basis for the Oder-Neisse Line. Since this was the situation in 1970,

did the Treaties of 1970 and subsequent events really change anything at all?

The conservative administration of Konrad Adenauer and his Christian Democratic Union (C.D.U.) remained in sole control of the West German Government until 1966, and foreign policy with respect to the Oder-Neisse Line remained unchanged. Still, with over twenty years of the Cold War having led to stagnation in Central Europe, there were voices in Germany and elsewhere that called for an effort to ease tensions between East and West. The 1966 elections in West Germany saw the C.D.U. lose its absolute control of the Bundestag, and from 1966 to 1969 the C.D.U. was forced to enter the Grand Coalition with the Bavarian Christian Social Union (C.S.U.) and the Social Democratic Party (S.P.D.), the latter headed by the liberal Willy Brandt. Brandt was part of a growing number of Germans who favored normalization of relations with the East Bloc at almost any price[1]. Brandt recognized that in order to establish diplomatic relations with Poland West Germany would have to recognize the inviolability of the Oder-Neisse Line from the standpoint of a guarantee that it would not be rectified by force, but only until such time as a peace treaty could be signed that would finally settle the problem[2]. Poland on the other hand considered the unconditional recognition by West Germany of the Oder-Neisse Line as the prerequisite for any type of diplomatic contact. The Soviet Union backed this stand fully, although the Soviet Union had had diplomatic contacts with West Germany since the 1950s. Negotiations with several East Bloc states, including the Soviet Union, began in the mid-1960s, but numerous stumbling blocks, especially the border issue, kept the Germans from making much progress. From 1966 to 1969 the C.D.U. adamantly refused to allow any discussion of recognition of the Oder-Neisse Line, and even most of the S.P.D. members, as well as a vast majority of the West German population, were opposed to giving up all claims to the Eastern Territories[3].

In 1969 the political situation in West Germany changed drastically when the S.P.D. under Willy Brandt won complete control of the Bundestag in conjunction with the Free Democratic Party (F.D.P). For the first time since the creation of the B.R.D. in 1949 the C.D.U. had become a minority opposition party and lost control over West German foreign policy. Still, the S.P.D. tried initially to carry on more or less the same policy as that followed by the C.D.U. Brandt was primarily interested in security, and tried to take part in an overall Western push for more dialogue with the Warsaw Pact. In a desire for European peace and cooperation and eventual German reunification the S.P.D. became willing to go further to accomodate Polish fears and desires[4]. Ostpolitik was given top priority in foreign policy matters, and West Germany took a certain

independence from N.A.T.O. in negotiations with the East that had not been attempted before. The S.P.D. desire for security required, in Brandt's eyes, some separation from reliance on N.A.T.O. and independent action.

Warmer relations were established with Romania even before the 1969 elections. Through Romania channels were opened with the Soviet Union, and after extensive negotiations in 1969 and early 1970 the Poles and Czechs finally agreed to hold meetings with West Germany[5]. The apparent break in West German foreign policy first appeared on May 22, 1970 when Germany and the Soviet Union jointly published a document on the results of their negotiations known as the Bahr Paper[6]. Article III of the Paper reads as follows:

> The Federal Republic of Germany and the Union of Soviet Socialist Republics share the realization that peace can only be maintained in Europe if nobody disturbs the present frontiers. They undertake to respect without restriction the territorial integrity of all states in Europe within their present frontiers. They declare that they have no territorial claims against anybody nor will they assert such claims in the future. They regard today and shall in future regard the frontiers of all states in Europe as inviolable such as they are on the date of signature of the present Treaty, including the Oder-Neisse line which forms the western frontier of the People's Republic of Poland...[7]

This statement was meant to give an indication to all concerned of the intention of the parties that would soon sign treaties normalizing relations. Opposition to the signing of the Treaties was extremely heavy in the Bundestag, and in order for the Bundestag to approve Brandt's actions at all he had to emphasize that these were non-aggression treaties, with the frontier inviolability provisions being merely guarantees that Germany would not change the frontier situation by force. As we shall see, the debates in the Bundestag on the ratification of the Treaties give the impression that most of the delegates never considered the Treaties to be a legal recognition of the cession of the Oder-Neisse Territories to Poland and the Soviet Union, and the Bahr Paper was considered an extreme effort at coming to an agreement with the East Bloc, and not the legal basis for the subsequent treaties[8].

On August 12, 1970 West Germany concluded with the Soviet Union the Treaty Between the Federal Republic of Germany and the Union of Soviet Socialist Republics (the Moscow Treaty). In Article II the parties agreed to "settle their disputes exclusively by peaceful means and undertake to refrain from the threat or use of force, pursuant to Article 2

of the Charter of the United Nations...". The crucial article is Article Three, which reads as follows:

> In accordance with the foregoing purposes and principles the Federal Republic of Germany and the Union of Soviet Socialist Republics share the realization that peace can only be maintained in Europe if nobody disturbs the present frontiers.
>
> • They undertake to respect without restriction the territorial integrity of all States in Europe within their present frontiers;
>
> • they declare that they have no territorial claims against anybody nor will assert such claims in the future;
>
> • they regard today and shall in future regard the frontiers of all States in Europe as inviolable such as they are on the date of signature of the present Treaty, including the Oder-Neisse line which forms the western frontier of the People's Republic of Poland and the frontier between the Federal Republic of Germany and the German Democratic Republic.[9]

Following closely upon this crucial treaty, West Germany concluded a similar treaty with Poland, which to many is the more important of the two for the Oder-Neisse question. On December 7, 1970 the Agreement between the Polish People's Republic and the Federal Republic of Germany Concerning the Basis for Normalization of Their Mutual Relations (Warsaw Treaty) was signed. Article I reads in full:

> 1. The Polish People's Republic and the Federal Republic of Germany agree that the existing frontier line, which, in accordance with chapter IX of the decisions of the Potsdam Conference of 2 August 1945, runs from the Baltic Sea immediately west of Swinoujscie along the Odra (Oder) River to the point of junction with the Nysa Luzycka (Lausitzer Neisse) River and along the Nysa Luzycka (Lausitzer Neisse) River to the frontier with Czechoslovakia constitutes the western State frontier of the Polish People's Republic.
>
> 2. They confirm the inviolability of their existing frontiers, now and hereafter, and pledge absolute respect for each other's territorial integrity.
>
> 3. They declare that they have no territorial claims against each other and will advance none in the future"[10].

At first reading the wording of these two treaties, especially the territorial provisions of the Warsaw Treaty, would seem to confirm unequivocally the annexation of the Oder-Neisse Territories by Poland and the Soviet Union. However, unlike a standard treaty of peace (which these are not) granting territorial transfers by the signed consent of the

parties, these two agreements are riddled with legal problems that present issues as complex as those relating to the Oder-Neisse Line before 1970.

The legal arguments of the West Germans in the post-1970 period have been accurately summed up by Dr. Surya Sharma:

> Federal Republic of Germany contends (a) that its commitment under the treaty bound just itself and not an all-German sovereign State which did not yet exist and hence cannot serve as a substitute for a peace settlement for the whole of Germany; (b) that the German-Polish treaty was not a frontier treaty in essence and its actual significance was depicted appositely as 'treaty concerning the basis for normalizing relations' and (c) that the rights and responsibilities of the Four Powers for Germany as a whole continued unchanged.[11]

The Polish counterclaims are also outlined:

> Poland takes the position (a) that the two German Republics, in their own right but also as successors or partial continuations of the Reich and, finally, as theoretical predecessors of a future unified Germany, have a legal interest in the boundaries; (b) that the territorial clauses of the treaty are unambiguous and they clearly express the Federal Republic's consent to the Oder-Neisse line; and (c) that most of the big powers have already recognized the Oder-Neisse line and in any case competence of four powers concerning "the peaceful settlement of the whole Germany" does not extend to the changing of the existing frontiers or to the dictation of new ones.[12]

These and some other lesser theories and problems will be addressed below. Before reviewing the wording and intention of the treaties themselves, we should first look to the application and legal standing of the treaties.

Perhaps the most often-debated question is the status of the B.R.D. and the D.D.R. Specifically, do they represent new international entities in the post-1945 world, or are one or both states the continuation in some fashion of the old German Reich? From 1949 to 1970 the B.R.D. maintained that it was the sole representative and successor of the German Reich, and was the only German state that could speak for the Reich. The D.D.R. maintained from its creation that it was not a successor to the old Reich, but was a new and independent state in the post-war world, with no claims or liabilities in the past[13]. While East Germany recognized West Germany as an equal from the start, even though West Germany refused to recognize East Germany as anything more than the "Russian Occupation Zone", she did not recognize West Germany's claim

to be the sole successor and spokesman for the German Reich. Of course, the problem with this long-standing West German claim is that if West Germany is the successor of the German Reich of 1937, then when it signed the treaties of 1970 it was signing them for the German Reich as a whole[14]. In fact, West German scholars and many Government officials have since claimed that West Germany was only empowered to sign the treaties on her own behalf, and these will thus not be binding on the united German Reich, when that nation is finally recreated[15]. During the Bundestag debates over the ratification of the Warsaw and Moscow Treaties Chancellor Brandt introduced the idea of a future all-German entity that would not be bound by the territorial status quo. Only after this idea was accepted by a majority of Members were the Treaties ratified, indicating the German interpretation of the Treaties as binding only upon the present provisional government[16].

Polish scholars challenge this by arguing the theory of state succession with respect to treaties, especially boundary treaties. The Poles argue that once the boundary is settled, which according to them was done in 1945 at Potsdam, the decision is irrevocable and unchangeable. The treaty is an executed, not an executory or continuously operating treaty, and thus its provisions are fulfilled and the treaty ended upon the establishment of the boundary. As the condition is already set, a successor state may not claim what has already been given away by the predecessor state[17]. The issue of states succeeding to treaties concluded by former sovereigns has received much attention since the colonial powers granted independence to many former colonies in the past thirty years, and each of these states came into existance burdened by treaties concluded by their former colonial masters, including many unequal treaties. This problem led recently to the signing by a number of states of the Convention on Succession of States in Respect of Treaties[18]. This Convention allows new or re-formed states to renounce treaties entered into by former sovereigns, especially in the case of former colonies. However, Article 11 states: "A succession of States does not as such affect: (a) a boundary established by a treaty; or (b) obligations and rights established by a treaty and relating to the regime of a boundary"[19]. Several writers have analyzed this problem in great detail. Jerzy Tyranowski believes that there are two main theories regarding succession to boundary treaties, both upholding the inviolability of a frontier, but for very different legal reasons. The first theory is that boundary treaties always devolve upon successor states due to their executory nature. The other theory is that a boundary treaty, also due to its executory nature, can not devolve upon a successor state, as it has already been fully performed, and thus there is nothing left to devolve; in essence the treaty dissappears after implementation[20]. As another writer

notes: "A state inherits certain rights and duties of its predecessor irrespective of anyone's will, including its own"[21]. This may indicate that even if West Germany states in signing the treaties that it could only sign on its own behalf, these treaties would still be binding on a successor. West Germany seems to have entered into a situation where its claimed legal status will cause the Oder-Neisse Territories to be legally separated. If West Germany is identical with the all-German Reich, as it has alleged in the past, then it can not deny that its treaties will apply to that state also[22]. On the other hand, if the all-German state is not now present in the form of West Germany, but is re-created later, it will be bound as a successor to the present state that signed the treaties. However, these conclusions do not spell the end of the Oder-Neisse controversy by any means.

First, the permanence of boundaries does not depend only upon a formalized and executed agreement, but also upon its validity. While there is a presumption in international law that a boundary is a definitive attribution of territory, "the doctrine of continuity of boundaries does not imply that in principle an illegal or invalid frontier must be perpetuated"[23].

Second, the B.R.D, contrary even to its own stated policy, may be neither identical with the old Reich nor the predecessor of a refounded all-German state. The B.R.D. was created by action of three of the Four Powers from occupation zones, in violation of the intentions of the Four Powers expressed earlier. Likewise the D.D.R. was created by unilateral action of the Soviet Union out of its one occupation zone. Both states came into being in 1949, and at least the D.D.R. claims to have no relation with past German states. While Germany was divided into zones of occupation in 1945 no part of these zones (except the Oder-Neisse Territories) was annexed or in any way taken over by another power. No declaration by any of the Allied nations subsequent to the German surrender in May, 1945 gave any indication of subjugation or annexation of any German territory, east or west of the Oder-Neisse[24]. Thus, even though German governmental functions ceased in May, 1945 (except on the local level), and the German military surrendered, the German Reich never legally ceased to exist[25]. It continued to exist under occupation from 1945 to 1949. When the B.R.D. was formed in 1949 it was considered to be a temporary situation until reunification and a peace treaty could be acheived. This is why the capital of the powerful B.R.D. is located in the small town of Bonn on the Rhine, instead of in a grand city designed for the purpose. Even the constitution of West Germany, the Basic Law, recognizes that eventually the law will be implemented in areas not presently under Western control[26]. When Germany is reunited it will not be an expansion of the B.R.D. or the D.D.R. Instead it will be the granting

of sovereign powers to the state that has lain dormant for over forty years. This state does indeed have all of the attributes of a sovereign state. It has territory, albeit under the occupation of two temporary German governments and four occupation powers (in the case of Berlin). Its governmental functions are still under the authority of the Four Powers, which exercise the authority that they took over in 1945, although today this is exercised directly only in Berlin (and effectively only in West Berlin). The authority of the Four Powers will be dealt with in more detail below. Suffice it here to say that the Four Powers and their delegated authorities, the governments of the B.R.D. and D.D.R, have kept the Reich alive. How could the situation be otherwise? In the period from 1945 to 1949 no annexation took place, so the Reich must have survived the War. The Reich still exists, and has not entered into any treaties renouncing claims to any territory.

One action that might change this situation is the conclusion of the Treaty on the Basis of Intra-German Relations on December 21, 1973[27]. In this treaty West Germany recognized the sovereignty of East Germany and the inviolability of her frontiers. Such recognition could mean the recognition of the treaties entered into by East Germany and also an admission that the B.R.D. is not the sole successor of the Reich or its only valid interim government[28]. However, as the Intra-German Treaty was concluded three years after the Warsaw and Moscow Treaties, it must be taken that the former legal status of the two Germanies was that under which the B.R.D. worked in negotiating the 1970 treaties. Furthermore, during negotiations over the Moscow and Warsaw Treaties Chancellor Brandt issued his "Twenty Points", which while advocating United Nations membership for the D.D.R, refused to recognize "the second state of Germany" under international law[29]. A suggestion has been made that the Inter-German Treaty may have not only legitimated the separate status of the two Germanies, but may have at the same time substantiated a single "Deutschland" that could conclude a boundary treaty for the nation. As such, the Eastern Treaties made by the B.R.D. were invalidated by this Treaty[30].

This leads us to one other interesting point. The B.R.D. had no ability to sign a treaty that would confirm the grant of the Oder-Neisse Territories to Poland. First, if the B.R.D. is to be considered a sovereign and new state within its own territory only, it does not even border on the Oder and Neisse, and thus could not give away such territory any more than it could grant Romanian territory to Bulgaria. More importantly, as several writers noted after the Gorlitz Agreement in 1950, the B.R.D., like the D.D.R, had no legal authority to sign away the Oder-Neisse Territories, or even to confirm their annexation, as the B.R.D. never

controlled them[31]! If the B.R.D. is one and the same with the old German Reich this might be a different matter. However, the same scholars who argue that the 1970 treaties are a valid action by the B.R.D. emphatically deny that the B.R.D. has any relation to the German Reich[32]. This would certainly be true if the treaties actually granted territory to another state. However, many persons argue that they merely confirm an annexation that already took place at Potsdam, and as we have seen, no such annexation ever became valid at Potsdam. In view of this, we come back to the conclusion that a future united Germany, a Reich re-emerged, must of legal necessity be endowed (at least initially) with the territory of the Reich of 1937.

> The general rule of customary international law in this matter is that, in principle, a state succeeds to the territorial limits of her predecessor: she gains no more and *no less* territory upon succession[33] (emphasis added).

The B.R.D. and D.D.R. had no legal standing to divest themselves of territory, so the pre-1945 boundaries will exist when these two entities are dissolved in favor of a united Germany.

An important problem related to the continued existance of the Reich, even if not a successor state, is the application of the *rebus sic stantibus* norm on the future frontier of the reunified Reich. This norm allows a state to change the terms and conditions of a treaty at a time after its signing if there is a "fundamental change of circumstances"[34]. However, Dr. Tadeusz Jasudowicz argues that like the state succession issue, a state may not apply this norm with respect to boundary treaties. Modern international law indicates that the primary interest of states is in the stability of frontiers, and thus a theory like this would allow states to demand rectification of frontiers after any change of circumstances, which would make most frontiers very elastic and unsteady. Also as in the case of state succession, Jasudowicz argues that as frontier treaties are executed treaties, there is nothing left to change later[35]. What this means is that when the Reich regains its sovereignty it will be bound to the Oder-Neisse Line if the 1970 treaties actually do grant sovereignty to Poland, even though there is an implication that frontiers could be changed by peaceful means. We shall see, however, that not only does this premise violate the basic national right to transfer title to territory by peaceful means and mutual consent, but in any event the title has not ever passed to Poland and the Soviet Union in the first place. We must delve into the language of the treaties to decide exactly what their effect is on the Oder-Neisse Territories. Before we do this, however, we must review the crucial role

that the Four Powers still play in Germany, the existance of which would prohibit a German-Polish treaty granting territory to Poland.

After the defeat of Germany in 1945 the four Allied Powers took up zones of occupation in Germany, with no outward intention of forming permanent separate states out of their zones. Later events would change this situation. Still, the Allies maintained a technical state of war with Germany until 1954 (for the Western Powers) or 1955 (for the Soviet Union). Great Britain, France and the United States maintained their military occupation of "Germany" until 1955. In that year they implemented a convention, signed in 1954 and known as the "Deutschlandvertrag", which reserved to the Four Powers (even though the Soviet Union did not participate) their rights relating to Germany as a whole until such time as a peace treaty could be signed[36]. A peace treaty has never been signed, and the rights of the Three Powers remain in force. One aspect of authority that the Four Powers had reserved for themselves as early as the Berlin Declaration in 1945 was the power to dispose of German territory and decide the frontiers[37]. This power was not given up in 1955, although control over administration and other government functions was handed over to the Germans[38]. The Soviet Union likewise retained similar prerogatives in East Germany under a unilateral declaration issued at the time of the "Deutschlandvertrag"[39].

Both in the wording of the 1970 treaties and in statements made by the West German Government before and after the signings it is clear that the reserved authority of the three Western Powers is recognized as limiting the effect of the treaties. Articles IV of the Warsaw Treaty[40] and the Moscow Treaty[41] specify that these treaties will not prejudice any agreements then in force that effect Germany, and letters sent to the Governments of Britain, the U.S. and France by West Germany assured them that these treaties would not have any effect on their rights and responsibilities in Germany[42]. In fact this was not just an attempt by West Germany to place conditions on the treaties, for the Three Powers insisted that the treaties must not affect their competences with respect to Germany[43].

The Poles contend that the Three Powers did not reserve authority to determine the frontiers after 1970. First, their reply letters to the German notes sent upon signing the treaties stated that they approved of the German action[44]. Subsequent action by these states would seem to indicate that they "recognized" the frontiers as set at Potsdam or by the 1970 treaties. Polish proponents argue that by recognizing the frontier the Western governments deprived themselves of the right of raising the issue at a peace settlement, should one ever take place[45]. As for an explanation of what rights were actually reserved in 1955 and again in 1970, many

scholars believe that control of Berlin (today only West Berlin), and the right to station troops in Germany are the last vestiges of Allied "rights" in Germany[46].

The problem with this argument is that while the Western Powers specifically gave up their other rights and responsibilities by declaration or treaty over the years (including the end of occupation in 1951 and the end of supervision of governmental entities in 1955), they have never renounced their right to determine territorial changes at a peace conference, and a renunciation of such magnitude can not be implied from silence. The current European situation may have led to a standoff between East and West, and made any thought of a peace settlement or proper handling of the German Problem unrealistic in the near future, but this does not change the legal status of the region. The 1970 treaties continue the tradition of reserving to the Western Powers their rights in Germany, and as of today those rights have yet to be renounced.

A related problem with the Great Powers is their general recognition of the territorial status quo in Europe. In international law a new situation, territorial or otherwise, may become legally binding if enough states recognize it. Some proponents claim that the letters of approval after the signing of the 1970 treaties were evidence of "recognition". On the other hand, the British Secretary of State noted after the treaties had been signed: "the British Government are glad to note that the German Government has come to this arrangement; but of course the final arrangement must await a final peace settlement of the German problem"[47]. In similar fashion the U.S. maintains that its position has not changed in the wake of the 1970 treaties, and the boundary provisions of the treaties would have to be accepted by the Allies, which would be done at the peace settlement. Until then the U.S. would not formally recognize the Oder-Neisse frontier[48].

In 1975 every state in Europe, plus the United States and Canada, entered into the Conference on Security and Cooperation in Europe held at Helsinki. The Final Act of the Helsinki Conference, signed by all participants, included provisions on territorial integrity and frontiers. Article 3 states:

> The participating States regard as inviolable all one another's frontiers as well as the frontiers of all States in Europe and therefore they will refrain now and in the future from assaulting these frontiers.
>
> Accordingly, they will also refrain from any demand for, or act of, seizure and usurpation of part or all of the territory of any participating state.[49]

Article 4 deals with territorial integrity of states:

> The participating States will respect the territorial integrity of each of the participating States.
>
> Accordingly, they will refrain from any action inconsistent with the purposes and principles of the Charter of the United Nations...and in particular from any such action constituting a threat or use of force.
>
> The participating States will likewise refrain from making each other's territory...the object of acquisition by means of such measures or the threat of them (military or other). No such occupation or acquisition will be recognized as legal.[50]

From the face of this document it would appear that all of the nations of Europe have recognized the territorial status quo. However, the Helsinki Final Act does not give any more legitimacy to the Oder-Neisse Line than it had prior to 1975. First, the Helsinki Act is not an international treaty and does not carry the weight of one[51]. Although some scholars believe that the Helsinki Act strengthened the territorial inviolability recognized in the 1970 treaties[52], from a purely legal point of view the most it can do is support the argument that the permanence of the present territorial makeup of Europe has become for Europe a norm of *jus cogens*. If anything the Helsinki Act may destroy the assumption that the 1970 treaties made the Oder-Neisse Line unchangeable and recognized the illegal annexation of 1945. In Article 1 of the Act it is stated that the parties "consider that their frontiers can be changed, in accordance with international law, by peaceful means and by agreement"[53]. Any argument that West Germany finally agreed to the frontiers of Europe when she signed the Helsinki Act is disproven by the fact that West Germany was the state that demanded that the provision relating to peaceful changes of frontiers be placed in Article 1. Furthermore, German scholars have protested the legality of various agreements between the B.R.D. and Poland relating to matters such as transportation and citizenship status, as they give the impression of not complying with West Germany's non-recognition of Polish sovereignty over the Oder-Neisse Territories[54]. Thus the territorial provisions of the Helsinki Act appear to be nothing more than a prohibition on the use of force or threat of use of force to make territorial changes. Helsinki is merely a European-wide non-aggression pact in this regard. And as Helsinki is such, so also the 1970 treaties appear to be merely non-aggression pacts, entered into by West Germany to better relations with the East Bloc without violating the rights of the Three Powers or changing the policy of refusing to recognize the permanence of the Oder-Neisse Line.

The wording of the 1970 treaties shows West Germany's clear intention of bettering relations without giving up the legal claim to the Oder-Neisse

Territories. Both treaties emphasize the renunciation of the use of force in their relations, and when this is read in conjunction with the provisions of territorial inviolability, the treaties become merely guarantees that Germany will not use force to rectify the border problem. The clear intention of the treaties as non-aggression pacts becomes obvious when one finds no provision that actually grants to Poland title to the Oder-Neisse Territories. Of course the Poles believe that these territories were legally handed over at Potsdam, a conclusion that has been disproven. West Germany never recognized the Potsdam Agreement as granting legal title to the Territories, and thus it would take a subsequent document to carry out this transfer. If the Warsaw Treaty does not accomplish this, then no treaty does. As even Polish proponents admit, the 1970 treaties do not in and of themselves give sovereignty over the Oder-Neisse Territories to Poland, and they could not have such legal effect. The only agreement that could do this is Potsdam[55].

Most German scholars consider the treaties as merely a *modus vivendi*, in effect not changing Germany's legal status vis a vis the Territories[56]. In the Moscow Treaty Article 2 relates only to the threat or use of force. Article 3 does not contain any territorial guarantee relating to the peaceful change of frontiers, as long as this would not violate Article 2 or the provisions of the Charter of the United Nations. Furthermore, nowhere in the Treaty is the Oder-Neisse Line specifically mentioned. The exact frontiers are never laid down, and no grant of territory is made. The Treaties only recognize the inviolability of "existing frontiers", and as Potsdam and Gorlitz did not validly transfer any territory, the "existing frontiers" of 1970 were those of 1945, i.e. inclusive of the Oder-Neisse Territories. The 1970 Treaties recognized a legal status that had never changed.

Finally, when the German Government signed the Moscow Treaty it transmitted to the Soviet Government a letter, which was accepted by the Soviet Union and thereby included in the treaty as an interpretive document, per Article 31(2)(a) of the Vienna Convention on the Law of Treaties, signed shortly before[57]. In this Letter on German Unity the West German Government made clear that the Moscow Treaty would not be interpreted to run against the basic German policies of reunification and determination of the frontiers on the basis of self-determination of peoples[58]. As one scholar has put it, "Bonn accepted the status quo with the declared intention to change it, if possible...The best way of knocking down frontiers may be to recognize them first"[59].

As for the Warsaw Treaty, this also appears to be merely a non-agression pact, for the frontier here is also not delimited, but is given a rather vague description. For a frontier to be stipulated as legally binding

in a treaty, it must be actually delimited in that treaty[60]. The inviolability provision must also be read in the context of non-agression. As one writer notes: "The inviolability of borders in the context of the non-use of force involves, principally, the prohibition to use force with the aim of violating existing borders and does not imply, necessarily, the recognition of the title and of all rights and obligations arising from the exercise of territorial sovereignty"[61]. This same writer agrees with a U.N. Declaration of 1970 that holds that states must refrain from the threat or use of force to change international boundaries. As he explains: "This does not affect the position of the interested states as regards the status and effects of such a line, resulting from its special regime, and does not alter the temporary nature of such a line"[62]. One scholar notes the distinction between the term "inviolable" used in the Treaty and the term "immutable" commonly used in boundary treaties. The former means only that the line could not be crossed without consent. The latter means that the line may never be changed[63]. It is also important to remember that "inviolability does not mean, of course, that cessions of territory or even a voluntary merger of the Federal Republic and the G.D.R. could be illegal under the treaty"[64].

To fully understand the exact West German interpretation of the 1970 treaties it is helpful to review the domestic cases and legislation of the B.R.D. While some scholars argue that "a party to a treaty cannot invoke provisions of its internal legislation as justification for its failure to perform the treaty"[65], still others believe that "The intention of the parties can be inferred either from the interpretation of the relevant legal instruments or through the conduct of the parties"[66]. In the case of the 1970 treaties it is crucial to review the legislation and court decisions in Germany because the West German interpretation of the treaties (which were initiated by West Germany), and thus its conduct toward them, has been uniform from the beginning. Between 1970 and 1972, during the debates prior to ratification of the treaties, opposition was strong. In the first vote in the Bundestag the treaties were actually defeated. Only after the official German interpretation of the treaties, outlined above, was agreed upon by the whole German Government were the treaties passed. The Soviet ambassador even took part in the debates over the treaties in West Germany, and Poland certainly knew about the German position[67].

On May 17, 1972 the Bundestag adopted by an overwhelming majority the Joint resolution on Foreign Policy. This Resolution indicated West Germany's desire to normalize mutual relations with the East Bloc, but declared it only an element of the "modus vivendi" with the East[68]. The Resolution went on to specify that the Treaties did not end West Germany's goal, and legal right, to modify the frontiers peacefully. Of course Poland does not consider the Resolution as having any weight

under international law, but at the same time some Polish writers consider that it has weakened the Warsaw Treaty[69].

Since 1970 German courts and legislatures have continued to act on assumptions present before the 1970 treaties in relation to the Oder-Neisse Territories. The German Constitution, or Basic Law, still contains Article 23, promising to extend the Basic Law to other German territories on their accession. The German Constitutional Court still maintains that the Reich exists within its borders as of December 31, 1937, and enjoys the rights of a subject of international law even though it has no power to act[70]. The Court has also recognized that while the Treaties may have caused the B.R.D. to recognize the Oder-Neisse Territories as foreign territories, no decision has been reached on the Reich's recognition of this situation. Before 1970 the Territories were *not* considered as foreign, and thus the 1970 treaties affect only the B.R.D., the Reich having no power to act in 1970 [71].

The German Government, irrespective of party control, continues to act on these assumptions. Chancellor Brandt's successor, Helmut Schmidt, wrote:

> The Federal Republic does not feel able to recognize formally and finally the Oder-Neisse Line as Poland's western border; this is a decision which even the architects of present-day Poland reserved to a peace treaty with Germany. But we are willing to do everything possible short of an eventual peace treaty. We have made the Poles a twofold offer: first, to concede in no uncertain terms that, in its view, the Oder-Neisse is the western frontier of Poland; and second, to commit itself to the inviolability of this frontier.[72]

A number of laws existed on the books in West Germany in 1970, and are still in effect today, that Poland claims are in contradiction of the spirit of the Warsaw Treaty. West Germany, however, sees no conflict between these laws and its interpretation of the Warsaw or Moscow Treaties, and thus has not moved to modify them. While there are probably dozens of different laws that somehow are related to the status of the Oder-Neisse Territories, a few examples will suffice for present purposes.

The Law on Citizenship of 22 February, 1955[73] holds that any person residing within "the territory of the German Reich as it existed on 31 December, 1937 (Germany)" is a citizen of the B.R.D. As one author points out, this might create an absurd result if ethnic Poles who moved into the Territories after 1945 were to begin to migrate to West Germany, or better yet Poles who had been born in the Oder-Neisse Territories since 1945 (meaning non-autocthon Poles) decided to become German citizens [74]. The law recognizes a common nationality for residents of both

the B.R.D. and the D.D.R, and the D.D.R. first adopted its own nationality law only in 1968. Thus only from 1968 could the Germans of the west and east constitute separate nationalities[75].Polish proponents consider any idea of a common German nationality as in conflict with the alleged status of the B.R.D. and D.D.R. as independent states[76]. The Law Concerning the Question of Expellees and Refugees of 19 May, 1953 [77] is even more thorough in its obvious application to the Oder-Neisse Territories. The law, which provides financial and other aid to expellees, applies not only to all persons who were resident in the Oder-Neisse Territories as of December 31, 1937 or before, but also to their spouses *and descendants*! This, as Polish writers have pointed out, gives the law a hereditary character that implies that even children born today are still to be considered expelled from their rightful homes in the east[78].

Polish and Russian proponents have declared that West German laws in conflict with the spirit of the 1970 treaties are invalid and should be modified accordingly, especially as the German Constitution also has a provision that requires German law to conform to international law[79]. However, this supports the contention that the German laws should be used to help define the German interpretation and purpose in signing the Treaties. The German Constitutional Court was established solely to scrutinize laws to determine their conformity with the Basic Law. It has not found the laws in question to be in violation of any provision of the Constitution, including the provision requiring conformity with international law. Furthermore, the Court has specifically held that this apparent recognition of the continued invalidity of the Polish-Russian annexation of the Oder-Neisse Territories is correct[80]. Because of these laws, and the records of Bundestag debates, many consider that the German interpretation of the 1970 Treaties has always been clear, and that the Oder-Neisse Line is still only a provisional, if long-term, situation[81].

The current German legal stand on the treaties has another implication. In 1928 the Permanent Court of International Justice ruled in the *Island of Palmas* Case that prescription may not begin running while any rival state maintains claims to the territory in question[82]. Current German laws, writings and court rulings all indicate that a very active German claim remains to the Oder-Neisse Territories, and Poland has no chance to obtain them by peaceful prescription, any more than by treaty[83].

At least one writer regards geographic elements, such as economic resources, strategic positions and communications routes, as partial legal justification for frontier changes[84]. Every major proponent of the post-1945 frontiers as set down by the Soviet Union and Poland has argued that the Oder-Neisse frontier is more easily defensible against future German

attacks. There is now a river separating the two states, and the frontier is much shorter, not surrounding Poland on three sides as it did before 1939. In addition, Poland has a much longer coastline that will make it more difficult for the Poles to be cut off from the outside world[85].

Some writers point out that the annexation of the Oder-Neisse Territories by Poland has given this state a self-contained transportation system, centered on the Oder River. One author argues that the Polish-Czech industrial region is a uniform and interdependent area that includes not only southern Poland around Cracow and central Czechoslovakia, but also *all* of Silesia, including the Oder River basin[86]. This is why the city of Stettin, situated west of the Oder River in the heart of Germany, was included in the Territories, as this city controls the mouth of the Oder River.

By far the most important geographic aspect of the frontier is economic. The Poles tried to get at the valuable mines and industries of Upper Silesia after World War One, but succeeded in obtaining only part of the area. The Upper Silesian region had always been divided between Germany and Poland or Russia, the boundaries having been set hundreds of years before industry took hold in that region. The coal seams, rivers that powered factories and provided transportation, and rail lines all crossed frontiers[87]. The unity of the region would provide a much stronger industrial base for the country that obtained it. In the field of agriculture the Poles also claimed that due to overpopulation they were in need of more land, and Pomerania and East Prussia would provide such land[88].

All of these arguments have merit, but most do not stand up to facts. Strategic considerations are certainly a factor, but with the many non-aggression agreements in Europe, and with modern weaponry, they are really anachronistic. The transportation line argument is also important, but the Oder-Neisse system was the only river serving Germany in the east, while Poland has the wide Vistula running through the heart of the country, able to serve all regions of Poland. The D.D.R. presently has no internal river transit system which it controls all the way to the sea. As for economic considerations, the Upper Silesian region was seen by Poles years ago as a way of turning their predominantly agricultural nation into a modern state. Evidence today indicates that the incorporation of the Silesian industries has done just that, while not dramatically affecting already over-industrialised Germany. On the other hand, the Poles also argue that the acquisition of more agricultural land (the Oder-Neisse Territories, except for Upper Silesia and the Baltic ports, were and are entirely agricultural) was of vital importance. This does not stand up to the facts. Since 1945 agricultural output in the Territories has dropped dramatically, and resettlement went very slowly. At the same time West

Germany was crowded with refugees from the east and had little agricultural land with which to feed them. Even today West Germany is grossly overcrowded and must import large amounts of agricultural products, while the Polish-occupied Territories are still underpopulated. Even the Polish press bewailed the terrible conditions and lack of productivity in the "Western Territories"[89]. A Danish writer who travelled through the Territories fifteen years after their occupation remarked that not even the basic industries had been rebuilt[90]. At the same time West Germany had already become the strongest nation in western Europe through its "Wirtschaftwunder", with industry and agriculture far exceeding pre-war production levels. On the other hand, Poland has gone from an agricultural exporter in 1938 to an importer in 1980, even though it gained substantial areas of fine farmland.

Lastly, there is the argument that Poland needed the Western Territories to settle the Polish population that was expelled (illegally) from lands east of the Curzon Line. However, statistics here indicate that this population could have been easily accomodated in a central Poland depopulated by the War, and in fact much land in Poland proper went untilled for many years after the War due to a lack of farm workers[91].

One last issue should be mentioned. The 1937 frontier between Germany and Poland was a line for the most part drawn in the Middle Ages. It was one of the most ancient and durable boundaries in Europe, even in the World, with strong historic and ethnic justification. Modern jurists are recognizing more and more that such boundaries may be unchangeable based upon these factors alone. With respect to Europe in particular Professor Verzijl has said that "the actual *trace* of many boundaries still dates back to feudal times...They appear to display a curious character of sacrosanctity which forbids their elimination even today"[92]. As we noted in the historical survey (above), German historic and ethnic claims to the Oder-Neisse lands run far deeper than those of any other claimant. The noted English jurist Ian Brownlie has said of such claims: "it would not be entirely correct to say that ethnological, tribal and traditional considerations were always ruled out in the settlement of boundary questions"[93]. If this is so, and it is a principle already applied in many areas of Asia and Africa, then the German right to the lands east of the Oder-Neisse becomes unassailable.

Notes

1. William Griffith, *The Ostpolitik of the Federal Republic of Germany,* 147-54 (1978).

2. Janicki, "Legal Problems Involved in the Realization by the Federal Republic of Germany of the Treaty with Poland Dated 7th December, 1970", 18 *Polish Western Affairs* 76, 82 (1977).

3. For the best account of early German negotiations with the East Bloc, as well as the intense debates in the Bundestag, see: Whetten, *Germany's Ostpolitik* (1971).

4. Griffith, *Supra*, at 173-181.

5. For a detailed account of the negotiation process with the East Bloc in 1969-70 see: Whetten, *Supra*.

6. Reprinted in full in: Whetten, *Supra*, Appendix I.

7. *Id*.

8. Griffith, *Supra*, and Whetten, *Supra*.

9. *Treaty Between the Federal Republic of Germany and the Union of Soviet Socialist Republics* (Moscow Treaty), August 12, 1970. 9 I.L.M. 1026 (Sept., 1970).

10. *Agreement Between the Polish People's Republic and the Federal Republic of Germany Concerning the Basis for Normalization of Their Mutual Relations* (Warsaw Treaty), December 7, 1970. 1972 U.N.T.S. 332; 10 I.L.M. 127 (Jan., 1971).

11. Surya P. Sharma, *International Boundary Disputes and International Law*, 136 (1976).

12. *Id*.

13. This is why East Germany refused to pay compensation to Israel for war losses sustained by European Jews at the hands of the Nazis.

14. Skubiszewski, "Zachodnia granica Polski w swietle ukladow z 1970 roku", 26 *Panstwo i Prawo* 476 (March-April, 1971).

15. See for example: Kimminich, "Die Ostvertrage", *Internationales Recht und Diplomatie* 15 (1970); Arndt, "rechtliche und politische Aspekte der deutschen Ostpolitik", 14 *Osterreichische Zeitschrift fur Aussenpolitik* 395 (1974).

16. Karl Kaiser, "The New Ostpolitik", (Hanreider, ed.) *West German Foreign Policy: 1949-1979*, 145, 150 (1980).

17. Skubiszewski, "Zachodnia granica..." *Supra*, at 481-87.

18. *Convention on Succession of States in Respect of Treaties* (Vienna Treaty Convention), August 13, 1978. Doc. A/CONF.80/31. While this Convention was written and signed a few years after the treaties here under discussion, it gives a general idea of the consensus of states on the practice of state succession to treaties, and thus its principles would be applicable to events in the same decade. Many writers will point out that the Vienna Convention was not, as of the early 1980s, binding international law, so its only value is as evidence of jus cogens. Tyranowski, "State Succession: Boundaries and Boundary Treaties", 10 *Polish Yearbook of International Law* 115, 133 (1979-1980).

19. Some writers consider that in the case of newly-independent colonial states even Article 11 can be waived, as they follow the principle of starting "with a clean slate". See: Tyranowski, *Supra*.

20. Tyranowski, *Supra*, at 116-120.

21. Skubiszewski, "Poland's Western Frontier and the 1970 Treaties", 67 *American Journal of International Law* 23, 27 (Jan., 1973).

22. Skubiszewski, "Poland's Western Frontier..." *Supra*, at 26.

23. Kaikobad, "Some Observations on the Doctrine of Continuity and Finality of Boundaries", 54 *British Yearbook of International Law* 119, 121 (1982).

24. In 1945 the four Allied Governments declared that the assumption of supreme authority did *not* affect the annexation of Germany. Frowein, "Legal Problems of the German Ostpolitik", 26 *International and Comparative Law Quarterly* 105 (Jan., 1974).

25. The courts of several European states have held that for legal purposes one Germany still exists as a state. *R. v. Bottrill ex parte Kuechenmeister* (1946) 1 All E.R. 635; Court of Appeal (1947) K.B. 41 (English Court); BGE 78, I, 124 (Swiss Federal Court).

26. Basic Law of the Federal Republic of Germany. As Amended Aug. 23, 1976. Article 23.

27. *Treaty on the Basis of Intra-German Relations* (Federal Republic of Germany - German Democratic Republic) (December 21, 1973) 22 I.L.M. 16.

28. Gelberg, "The Case of the Treaty Concerning the Bases of Relations between the GDR and the FRG", 15 *Polish Western Affairs* 259 (1974).

29. Albert, "Bonn's Moscow Treaty and Its Implications", 49 *International Affairs* 316, 319 (1971).

30. Oppermann, "Das Ende der Bundesrepublik Deutschland?", *Internationales Recht und Diplomatie* 153 (1972).

31. It is interesting to note that the D.D.R. has never signed a treaty with the Soviet Union recognizing the annexation of the Königsberg region, for it never bordered on this territory either.

32. Skubiszewski, "Nowe traktaty w sprawach niemieckich: problemy terytorialne", 28 *Panstwo i Prawo* 13 (May, 1973); Kimminich, "Ostvertrage", *Supra*.

33. Kaikobad, *Supra* at 126.

34. Jasudowicz, "The Prohibition to Apply the *rebus sic stantibus* Norm with Respect to Treaties Establishing National Frontiers", 8 *Polish Yearbook of International Law* 155 (1976); see also: Kaikobad, *Supra*, at 129-130.

35. Jasudowicz, *Supra* at 166ff.

36. *Convention Between the United Kingdom, the United States, France and the Federal Republic of Germany on Relations Between the Three Powers and the Federal Republic of Germany*, (Oct. 23, 1954). 331 U.N.T.S. 328. Art. 2.

37. Skubiszewski, "The Great Powers and the Settlement in Central Europe", 18 *Jahrbuch fur Internationales Recht* 92, 96 (1975). For a detailed analysis of the Berlin Declaration of 1945 see the previous chapter in this work. A similar article is: Skubiszewski, "Les Traites sur les Frontieres en Europe Centrale (1970-73)", 6 *Polish Yearbook of International Law* 7 (1975).

38. It is also interesting to note that in 1955 the Western Powers began to speak of a "negotiated" peace settlement with Germany, rather than a dictated settlement, inferring that all of the interested parties would give their consent to the final boundary settlement. Skubiszewski, "The Great Powers...", *Supra*, at 106.

39. Skubiszewski, "The Great Powers...", *Supra*, at 101.

40. 1972 U.N.T.S. 332.

41. 9 I.L.M. 1026

42. Texts of these identical letters are appended to copies of the treaties. See: 1972 U.N.T.S. 332; 9 I.L.M. 1026.

43. Kimminich, "Ostvertrage", *Supra*; Skubiszewski, "The Great Powers..." *Supra*, at 104. These letters are most important for challenging any Polish prescriptive claims. Prescription may not begin as long as title to territory is disputed. Diplomatic correspondence has been held by the International Court of Justice to constitute sufficient notice of dispute. *Interpretation of Peace Treaties with Bulgaria, Hungary and Romania* (Advisory Opinion). (1950) I.C.J. 65, 221. One writer argues that the wording of the Allied agreement goes back to the theory of the B.R.D. as a successor to the Reich: "It is made clear thereby that the Federal Government acted only for the Federal Republic of Germany and that the question of the boundaries of a reunited Germany was not the object of negotiations". Frowein, *Supra*, at 120.

44. Replies to the German notes are attached with the notes. Skubiszewski, "The Great Powers...", *Supra*, at 104.

45. Skubiszewski, "Poland's Western Frontier...", *Supra*, at 30.

46. Skubiszewski, "The Great Powers...", *Supra*, at 108ff.

47. Frowein, *Supra*, at 112, n.39.

48. *Id*.

49. *Final Act of the Conference on Security and Cooperation in Europe* (Helsinki Conference), August 1, 1975. Reprinted in full in: Igor Kavass, *Human Rights, European Politics, and the Helsinki Accord*, at 185 (1981).

50. *Id*.

51. Symonides, "The Inviolability of the Frontiers and the Territorial Integrity in the Treaties between Poland and the GDR, between Poland and the FRG, and in the Final Act of the Helsinki Conference", 11 *Polish Yearbook of International Law* 25, 42 (1984). See also: Korey, *Human Rights and the Helsinki Accord*, 20-22 (1983).

52. *Id*.

53. Helsinki Final Act, Article 1, *Supra*.

54. Arndt, "Zu einigen Rechtsproblemen der deutsch-polnischen Vereinbarungen von 1975", 13-14 *Zeitschrift fur Recht und Politik* 1 (1977-78).

55. Janicki, *Supra*, at 84.

56. Arndt, *Die Vertrage von Moskau und Warschau* (1973).

57. 8 I.L.M. 679 (1969).

58. Steinberger, "Volkerrechtliche Aspekte des deutsch-sowjetischen Vertragswerks vom 12 August 1970", 31 *Zeitschrift fur Auslandisches Offentliches Recht und Volkerrecht* 63, 147 (1971).

59. Albert, *Supra*, at 316.

60. Skubiszewski, "Poland's Western Frontier...", *Supra*, at 36.

61. Symonides, *Supra*, at 33.

62. Symonides, *Supra*, at 38. Many writers consider the 1970 treaties as merely "renunciation of force" agreements, and these treaties are more often cited as part of the European move away from military solutions to international disputes. See for example: Korey, *Supra* at 13; Albert, *Supra*, at 32.

63. Albert, *Supra*, at 323. Another writer notes that in the Moscow Treaty the German text contains the word "Unverletzlichkeit", which translates "inviolability", while the Russian text uses the word "nerushimye", meaning "unchangeable". Frowein, *Supra*, at 109, n.25.

64. Frowein, *Supra*, at 109.

65. Gelberg, "The Warsaw Treaty of 1970 and the Western boundary of Poland", 76 *American Journal of International Law* 119 (January, 1982).

66. Sharma, *Supra*, at 136.

67. Ortmayer, *Conflict, Compromise, and Conciliation: West German-Polish Normalization: 1966-1976*, 83-94 (1975).

68. Skubiszewski, "Poland's Western Frontier...", *Supra*, at 33.

69. *Id*.

70. Gelberg, *Supra*, at 120. See: 36 BVerfGE 1, 16 (1974).

71. Arndt, "Legal Problems of the German Eastern Treaties", 74 *American Journal of International Law* 122, 129 (Jan., 1980).
See: 40 BVerfGE 141 (1976).

72. Schmidt, "Germany in the Era of Negotiations", *Foreign Affairs*, 40 (Oct., 1970).

73. Gesetz uber die Staatsangehorigkeit vom 22 Februar 1955, BGB1., part I, P.431.

74. Jasica, "The Legislation of the Federal Republic of Germany and the Problem of Normalization of Mutual Relations between the Polish People's Republic and the Federal Republic of Germany",7 *Polish Yearbook of International Law* 77 (1975).

75. Frowein, *Supra*, at 123. Dr. Frowein rightly points out that the existence of a nationality is one of the elements of statehood. Does this mean that the D.D.R. may not have been able to claim statehood before 1968?

76. Janicki, "The Territory and State Citizenship in the Legal Systems of the German Democratic Republic and the German Federal Republic", 12 *Polish Western Affairs* 44 (1971).

77. Gesetz uber die Angelegenheiten der Vertriebenen und Fluchtlinge (Federal law on Expellees) vom 19. Mai 1953, BGB1., part I, P.201. This law was amended, but not relevent to this discussion, on July 27, 1957, June 29, 1961 and September 19, 1961. See: Jasica, *Supra*, at 79.

78. Jasica, *Supra*, at 100. After the Warsaw Treaty was ratified a move was made to change this law, and persons from the Territories were still considered German as they had been before 1970, and before 1945. Thus the Treaties had no effect on nationality, a key element of state possession. Kimminich, "Der Warschauer Vertrag und die Staatsangehorigkeit der 'Polen-Deutschen'", 24 *Die Offentliche Verwaltung* 577 (1971).

79. Grundgesetz, Article 4. For an argument against the German laws, see: Jasica, *Supra*.

80. 36 BVerf GE1, 16 (1974).

81. Kaiser, *Supra*, at 154. See also: Johnson, "Acquisitive Prescription in International Law" 27 *British Yearbook of International Law* 332 (1950).

82. *Island of Palmas Case* (United States v. Netherlands). P.C.I.J. (1928).

83. MacGibbon, "The Scope of Acquiescence in International Law", 31 *British Yearbook of International Law* 143 (1954) supports the notion that domestic laws, case decisions and parliamentary actions and statements are proof of a lack of acquiescence in an international boundary situation.

84. Bognar, "Politicko-Geografske i Geopoliticke Osobine Granica Poljske", 19 *Jugoslovenska Reviija za Mesunarodno Pravo* 36 (1972).

85. See for example: Jordan, *The Oder-Neisse Line* (1952); Drzewieniecki, *The German-Polish Frontier* (1959).

86. Jordan, *Supra*, at 87-96.

87. Pounds, *The Upper Silesian Industrial Region*, (1958).

88. Kruszewski, *The Oder-Neisse Boundary and Poland's Modernization*, (1972).

89. Goettinger Research Committee, *The German Eastern Territories in Light of the Polish Press*, (1958). Lest the reader believe that these accounts are out of date, the author's personal visit to the Oder-Neisse Territories in 1985 confirmed that over forty years after the Territories were occupied by Poland they are still in low productivity, with much fallow land and low-density habitation.

90. Wassermann, *Europe's Forgotten Territories*, (1960).

91. Kruszewski, *Supra*.

92. Quoted in: Kaikobad, *Supra*, at 133-34.

93. Ian Brownlie, *African Boundaries: A Legal and Diplomatic Encyclopaedia*, 8 (1979).

5

THE EXPULSION OF THE GERMAN POPULATION FROM THE ODER-NEISSE TERRITORIES

The greatest tragedy of the Oder-Neisse controversy is not that a sovereign nation was deprived of almost one-third of its territory in violation of recognized norms of international law. While this was indeed a great injustice perpetrated upon the German nation as a whole, the fate that befell the German inhabitants of this territory was both a violation of international law and a crime against humanity.

Commencing some months before the conclusion of hostilities, Russian and Polish authorities began to expel German inhabitants from their homes in the territories occupied by their armies. At the conclusion of hostilities in May, 1945 but before the Potsdam Conference these two powers set in motion the wholesale and systematic expulsion of Germans living east of the Oder-Neisse Line. This action continued unabated (except for a few weeks during the Potsdam Conference) for the next three years, with smaller expulsions taking place until the end of the decade. Such actions were taken in violation of specific Allied agreements, including the Potsdam Accords that were being signed at precisely the same time, and established principles of international law. What made the situation even more intolerable was the inhumane manner in which it was accomplished. The inhabitants were subjected to extreme personal abuse, seizure of all of their property, and wholesale slaughter. At the same time the Allies were comdemning Nazi Germany for perpetrating the same crimes against others. The manner of the Expulsions, as well as the Expulsions as a policy, violated numerous norms of international law and

civilized humanity. This was indeed the final genocide of World War Two. Today the victims of this, the greatest mass expulsion of a people in modern history, have yet to be vindicated, much less compensated, for this gross violation of their rights. Even more than the boundary issue, this facit of the Oder-Neisse Problem brings forth established principles of international law that unequivocally condemn the actions of the Soviet Union and Poland.

Russian troops did not reach German territory until the autumn of 1944. In September the great Soviet offensive that had crushed Army Group Center in Byelorussia rolled to the borders of East Prussia. Numerous Russian units crossed on to German soil for the first time. Most Germans living on the East Prussian frontier remained in their villages, either out of ignorance of the impending danger or in obediance to orders issued by the Gauleiter of East Prussia, Erich Koch, that no one was to evacuate. As a consequence the advancing Russian units found the Prussian villages fully inhabited. German counterattacks pushed most of the Russians out of East Prussia by November, and what they found in the liberated villages of eastern East Prussia was to be only a precursor of what was to come. In the town of Nemmersdorf close to the frontier, the entire population, mostly old men, women and small children, had been slaughtered. Many had been shot outright, but the women were subjected to bestial horrors. Several were found crucified on barn doors. Babies had their heads beaten in, and others were obviously tortured to death. After the Red Cross was invited to visit the site they issued a report condemning this atrocity[1]. Despite this, the fate of Nemmersdorf would be replayed in thousands of German towns in the months ahead.

The attitude of the invading Soviet and Polish troops is at least partially understandable. Their countries had been subjected to four to six years of brutal Nazi administration in which millions of Russians, Poles and other Slavs and Jews were systematically deported for slave labor or massacred. Vast stretches of European Russia were laid waste, and almost every Russian and Polish soldier had lost several loved ones. The desire for revenge was innate in the soldiers as they entered German territory for the first time. This deep emotion was exploited by the Soviet and Lublin Polish Governments, which made no attempt to control the fanaticism of their troops. The most notorious Soviet propagandist, Ilya Ehrenburg, wrote numerous articles and pamphlets, published in Soviet Army newspapers, that called for the wholesale extermination of the German population[2]. One particularly hateful tract called on the Russian troops to rape, plunder and kill at will, as this was not only their right but also their duty to the Motherland and their dead relatives[3]. Such policies were readily encouraged by Soviet military and political officers at the front,

many of whom looked the other way while their men rampaged through a captured village. There are, of course, accounts of the kindness of some Soviet officers, who forbid their men to take excesses with the local population, and at times would protect German women by force of arms from their own men[4].

After the Soviet 1944 Offensive was stalled in November, the Russian Army and its Polish allies regrouped on the East Prussian frontier and the Vistula. This gave the Germans time to evacuate at least some of the population, but few people left their homelands. In some areas local Nazi Party officials refused to allow any evacuations, still believing in the invincibility of the German Army[5]. Even moreso, the local population had such a deep attachment to its homeland that even in the face of impending Russian occupation many refused to leave[6]. There is substantial support for the argument that the excesses committed by the invading Soviet armies were calculated to do more than exact revenge on the Germans. Such an obviously systematic policy was intended to do no less than scare the native population out of the Oder-Neisse Territories, in preparation for their planned annexation by Poland and the Soviet Union. This would allow the Soviets to get around the provisions of the Atlantic Charter and the World consensus that territorial changes would have to conform with the freely-expressed will of the inhabitants. If the Russians could eliminate most of the German population in the Oder-Neisse Territories during the War then their annexations could be better justified. This theory was at least partially proven during the Potsdam Conference in July, 1945. During discussions concerning the Oder-Neisse frontier, President Truman expressed concern about the large German population in the Oder-Neisse Territories and the rights of the population to its homeland. Stalin informed him that this was not a problem, as there were no Germans left in the Territories (a clear lie). Upon hearing this Admiral Leahy, one of Truman's aides, pointedly remarked: "Of course not, the Bolshies have killed all of them!"[7].

The final Soviet offensive against Germany commenced on January 11th, 1945. The overwhelming numbers of Soviet and Polish troops quickly broke through German lines on the Vistula and Narew Rivers and on the eastern frontier of East Prussia. The shattered remnants of the German Army could not hope to stop the Russian advance. By the last week of January all of Poland had been liberated, German forces in East Prussia had been cut off from the rest of Germany in a giant pocket, all of Silesia east of the Oder had been overrun and Soviet tanks were on the banks of the Oder in East Brandenburg, scarcely forty miles from Berlin. During February most of the rest of Silesia was overrun, except for the mountainous regions and the fortress of Breslau. Soviet forces also

approached Danzig and were reducing the Heiligenbeil pocket in East Prussia, leaving Königsberg and the Samland Peninsula as the last German outpost there[8]. In all of these areas systematic brutality by the invading armies was the order of the day. Many Germans who were allowed or chose to evacuate at the last minute were caught on their treks by advancing Russian units and suffered the same fate as if they had remained at home, namely plunder, rape and mass slaughter[9].

East Prussia was the first province to be substantially occupied by the Russians. In less than a month from the start of the Soviet offensive the Germans were reduced to control of a pocket of territory around the Frisches Haff, centered on Heiligenbeil, plus Königsberg and the Samland Peninsula. When Soviet troops occupied Elbing on February 10th after a violent siege they isolated East Prussia by land from the rest of Germany [10]. Thousands of refugees fleeing the swift Russian advance clogged the roads and hindered German troops moving to the front. Many had left their homes on hours notice and travelled by horse-drawn cart or on foot, carrying only the barest essentials. Their plight was made worse by the extreme winter conditions then prevailing in eastern Europe. Few East Prussians managed to flee to central Germany by land, as the Russian advance had cut them off. Instead many were packed into the Heiligenbeil pocket and Königsberg. As the Russians closed in, these refugees headed across the frozen Frisches Haff to the long Frisches Nehrung and the ice-free ports of Pillau and Danzig. From here German naval and merchant ships evacuated as many persons as they could[11]. After Pomerania was overrun in March and Danzig was besieged hundreds of thousands of civilians and soldiers were evacuated by sea from the Bay of Danzig as well as the Hel Peninsula and Pillau. German troops managed to maintain a bridgehead in this area until the general surrender of all German forces on May 9th. During this time the heroism of the German Navy allowed many refugees to be evacuated to the West instead of falling into Russian hands[12].

Those Germans who remained in their homes faired even worse. Not only were the usual plunderings, rapings and shootings experienced, but many able bodied men and women were deported to the Soviet Union for forced labor, not to return for ten years[13]. Soon after, while the war was still progressing, Russian military administrators were replaced by Polish and Russian civilian authorities, who ordered many Germans to abandon their homes and farms[14]. These were promptly occupied by Polish and Russian settlers, and most personal property was also handed over to these new residents[15]. When the City of Danzig was taken on March 30th the entire population was immediately expelled to the West or sent to labor camps in Siberia. The fortress of Königsberg held out until April 9th.

When the remains of this devastated royal city were occupied many inhabitants were retained to work as forced labor, but were immediately expelled from their homes and forced to live on almost no food, in unheated barracks, for months. The City's Volksturm were shot en mass, and its regular army defenders spent ten years in Siberia[16].

Similar stories emerged from Silesia. Here too the Russians and Poles began to expel the majority of Germans who chose to remain in their homes, and many died on the long treks west. The remaining Germans were forced to work for Polish settlers who began to arrive several months before the end of hostilities. They also lost their homes and all possessions[17]. Endless accounts of the brutality perpetrated by the Polish administrators in Silesia indicate again the intentional policy of scaring the German inhabitants out of the territory[18]. A substantial number of refugees from eastern Silesia merely trekked to the Sudeten Mountains, which were not occupied until after the end of hostilities. Many more were trapped in the City of Breslau, which suffered a four-month siege and only capitulated on May 6th, six days after Berlin[19].

By April 1 all of the Oder-Neisse Territories had been overrrun, except for small pockets of resistance. Streams of refugees were arriving in central Germany and Bohemia, where their plight could scarcely be assuaged. On May 9th the German armed forces surrendered, and all of Germany fell under Allied occupation. At this time, two months before the Potsdam Conference, a tremendous number of Germans remained in the Oder-Neisse Territories, and many more began returning home from other parts of central Europe. In May and June an untold number of refugees returned to their homes east of the Oder-Neisse, despite the hostility of the Soviet and Polish administrators. While the chaotic circumstances made any figures impossible to obtain, it is probably accurate to say that the majority of Germans who fled before the advancing Russian Army returned to the Eastern Provinces after hostilities ceased. Some estimate over 1,500,000 Germans who had fled earlier actually managed to return to their homes[20].

It was at this point that the Russian and Polish Governments instituted a policy that has become one of the grossest violations of human rights perpetrated in peacetime. In June refugees returning from the west found their crossings at the Oder and Neisse Rivers were blocked by Polish militia. At the same time Russian occupation authorities were handing over all governmental functions in the Territories to officials from the Lublin Polish Government (except in northern East Prussia, where Soviet civilian officials took over). Many of the larger cities had already seen their German inhabitants expelled, either to the countryside or to the West. Now the Poles began the systematic expulsion of the entire German

population in the Oder-Neisse Territories. In each village and town Polish officials would move in and with Russian Army assistance demanded that the German inhabitants evacuate their dwellings, usually with no more than one hour's notice. Those that were not shipped to the Soviet Union for forced labor were sent west. Polish and Russian settlers occupied the German's dwellings and took their personal property[21]. As the expellees trekked west they were usually robbed of all of their remaining possessions, and sometimes raped, beaten or even killed by Polish brigands, militia and even regular Soviet soldiers. Thousands died on the treks west, probably no less a number than in the wartime treks. Many of these unfortunates had just returned after fleeing from the War, and were now forced to trek for the second time. By the time these people had made it to reception camps in central and western Germany they were starved, beaten, vermin-infested and utterly destitute.

The expulsions were carried out in an obviously pre-planned and systematic manner. In the summer of 1945 the people of the eastern and central districts of Silesia and Pomerania, plus the remaining Germans of West Prussia, were expelled. This occurred *before* the meeting of the Potsdam Conference, which the Poles and Russians would later use to justify the expulsions. The plight of the expellees so horrified the Western leaders that Churchill specifically lodged a complaint with Stalin at Potsdam, as did Truman later[22]. In the interest of maintaining good relations the Soviets halted the expulsions in July. However, after the Potsdam Conference ended the expulsions continued as before, this time with western Pomerania and Silesia and East Brandenburg being "cleaned out". As the severe winter of 1945 came on the death toll among expellees rose enormously, and with it World outcry against the manner and fact of the expulsions[23]. The expulsions were temporarily stopped for the winter.

In the spring of 1946 the largest expulsions were carried out, and smaller expulsions continued until 1949. In many areas the Germans were kept on until towns had been rebuilt and fields replanted, then they were summarily expelled. In every case the people were thrown out with little more than the clothes on their backs, and had not received proper food or medical care in months or years. The new Polish and Russian inhabitants treated the Germans as little more than slaves, although again there are many stories of kindness being extended by sympathetic Poles[24].

In northern East Prussia the Russian administration kept the German population of Königsberg working on removing rubble until 1948, when all Germans were expelled from the City. During captivity in their own city the Königsberg Germans lived in bombed out shelters on the sparcest rations for three years. They were probably luckier than the men and women who had been shipped to Siberia for forced labor, for many of

those never returned[25]. While the expulsions from Polish-occupied Germany occurred over time and were far from complete, the Russianization of northern East Prussia ranks as the quickest and most complete change of the culture of a territory in modern history. In 1946 the name of Königsberg was changed to Kaliningrad, and soon other town names were changed to names unrelated to the region. Settlers from the Ukraine, Byelorussia and Russia proper were moved into the territory, and in 1948 every single German in northern East Prussia was expelled, along with ethnic Masurians and Lithuanians who had lived under German suzereignty. Every geographic point and place name was Russianized, and by 1950 there was no trace of the thousand-year German habitation, other than the architecture of the remaining buildings[26].

In the 1950s the Polish Government claimed to have no ethnic Germans remaining in its territory, but this is belied by the facts. Many multilingual Germans chose to pass themselves off as Poles to avoid being expelled from their homes after 1945. Still others, due to technical knowledge or other traits useful to the Polish Government, were forced to accept Polish nationality and were not allowed to leave[27]. Many half-Germans, Masurians and other non-Polish minorities were left as is by the Poles. As such a substantial population of Germans, the numbers will never be known, still resides in the Polish occupied territories. Many travellers to the region in the 1950s and 1960s reported coming across whole villages of ethnic Germans[28]. Today a new generation has grown up that in many cases can not speak the German language, but still remains ethnically German. It is estimated that well over one million Germans still live in the occupied territories, although after 1970 freer Polish emmigration laws brought another waive to the West[29]. While the Poles keep insisting that no more Germans reside in the Territories, in 1988 a large waive of "German Poles" arrived in West Germany, many unable to speak German but most carrying German names and an affinity for the German culture of the pre-1945 east[30].

There is no way that we shall ever determine the exact number of people who were expelled from their homes, although it is readily admitted that the expulsion of the German population from the Oder-Neisse Territories was "the greatest forcible dislocation of persons in European history"[31]. According to reliable statistics, in 1939 the German population of the Territories numbered about 9,575,000 persons, including 2,473,000 in East Prussia, 1,884,000 in Pomerania, 642,000 in East Brandenburg and 4,577,000 in Silesia. In addition there were 380,000 Germans in Danzig and over 100,000 in the Memel Territory[32]. During the War the region suffered approximately 1,100,000 casualties[33]. At the end of 1944 there were an estimated 10,312,000 Germans permanently resident

in the Oder-Neisse Territories and Danzig plus several million more temporarily residing there[34]. After several air raids on large cities, the Russian front ravaged the area in the winter and spring of 1945, and the first refugees fled and tried to return, the population of the Territories at the end of the War was estimated to be roughly 10,000,000[35].

Exact tallies on the number of persons expelled and/or killed are not possible, in that the situation remained chaotic for several years, and most records in the east were destroyed. At best estimate, between 1945 and 1950 some 8,169,000 Germans were expelled from the Oder-Neisse Territories. Of these 1,101,000 perished on the trek[36]. Approximately 4,000,000 had migrated to East and West Germany in 1945, with another 4,000,000 coming between 1946 and 1950[37]. By 1950 West Germany had received 891,000 from Pomerania, 1,347,000 from East Prussia, 131,000 from East Brandenburg and 2,053,000 from Silesia. In addition 225,000 former Danzig residents and 48,000 Germans from Memel resided in West Germany[38]. An additional 4,000,000 Germans from the Territories had settled in East Germany.

Added to this mass of humanity fleeing west were German expellees from other parts of Europe. Communist regimes set up in East European countries decided to follow the policies of Poland and the Soviet Union with respect to their German minorities. Czechoslavakia expelled 2,921,000 Germans in 1945, most from the Sudetenland, in a brutal manner that rivalled even the Poles. Most were loaded onto sealed freight cars or forced to trek over the Sudeten Mountains on foot, suffering the usual plunder, rape, murder and beatings[39]. Simultaneous expulsions were also undertaken in Hungary, Romania, Yugoslavia, Bulgaria, and the Soviet occupied Baltic States, with some 1,865,000 Germans arriving from these countries and 613,000 dying along the way[40]. By 1955 there were over 13,000,000 expellees living in Germany and Austria, most in West Germany[41]. At this time there were still over 72,000 known to be prisoners in the Soviet Union, plus an untold number of unaccounted-for refugees. Every one of these expellees arrived after a brutal journey, with no property or resources in most cases except the clothing on their backs and in various stages of sickness and exhaustion[42]. All had to be absorbed by a nation that was completely devastated by the War and had an indigenous population to house and feed. What is more, before the War the Oder-Neisse Territories produced enough food for 15,400,000 people, enough to feed their entire population plus yielding a surplus to feed 5,800,000 people in other parts of Germany. In 1950 West Germany not only lacked this food surplus, for the Poles refused to send any agricultural products west, but was also forced to feed almost 13,000,000 additional people, making Germany for the first time a large net food importer[43]. All in all,

this was one of the greatest tragedies to have befallen a people in recorded history. What is more, the entire saga, from planning to execution, was in complete violation of international law as recognized both then and now.

The idea of removing the German population from Polish land was, like the idea of giving German territory to Poland, discussed very early in the War. During a meeting of the Inter-Allied Council in London on September 24, 1941 Polish Minister Raczynski stated: "the Polish population of the Western Provinces, so ruthlessly transplanted, must be given a possibility of an immediate reintegration in the land of their ancestors; and the German settlers, installed in Polish homesteads, sent back to the Reich."[44]. At this time there had been no serious discussions concerning the transfer of pre-1939 German territory to Poland. After the German conquest of Poland in 1939 the former Prussian provinces of Posen and West Prussia were reannexed to the Reich, along with a portion of central Poland known as the Warthegau. Many Poles were moved out of these predominantly Polish territories and settled in the General Gouvernment, the rump state of Poland set up by the Germans around Lublin. Simultaneously a great number of German settlers were moved into the former Polish lands. These joined the large German minority already resident in Poland proper, estimated in 1939 to constitute some 1,371,000 persons[45]. The question that emerges from of this set of facts, and remains one of the most crucial to the whole issue of the expulsions, is exactly which German settlers were *meant* to be expelled after the War, and especially which Germans the Western Allies intended to expel? As we shall note below, there is strong evidence to suggest that the Western Allies only acquiesced in the expulsions because they believed that they were limited to those Germans living in Poland proper. This group was viewed as a potential "fifth column" threat to Poland's security. Had they known that the Poles and Russians intended to expel millions of Germans from traditional German territory, they would never have accepted the principle of expulsions in wartime agreements or thereafter.

The idea of the transfer of populations was first discussed by the Allied leaders at the Teheran Conference in 1943. Stalin suggested that all Germans resident in territory to be annexed by Poland should be sent to Siberia or South America[46]. All seemed to acquiesce in principle to population transfers, but no formal agreement was reached at Teheran. In any event the exact amount of territory to be ceded had not even been discussed, so the determination of which German residents to expel would necessarily be premature. No distinction was made between Germans in German territory to be annexed and those who were residents of other countries, such as Poland and Czechoslavakia.

That the idea of mass expulsions was not being seriously considered by all of the Allies (we shall never know how early the Soviets and Poles began planning for the event) soon became apparant. The next discussion of the matter came in December, 1944, recorded in a telegram from the U.S. Ambassador in Moscow to Secretary of State Stettinius. In it he reported on talks held with the Lublin Poles and Mikolajczyk in October. They had agreed that "they did not wish any German population to remain within **Polish territory** because of the acute minority problem that this would create. The Russians and British accepted this principle"[47]. The Ambassador noted that Churchill had recently made a speach in which he advocated some population transfers after the War, and further that Dr. Benes of Czechoslavakia had obtained Stalin's support for the removal of some or most of the Sudeten Germans[48]. The Lublin Polish Government had advocated the mass removal of the German population from an early date. In August 1944 their foreign minister, Osobka-Morawski, announced a policy "to remove all Germans from the new Poland, except those required temporarily for reconstruction and those whose Polish-Masurian origin had been obscured by Germanization, for many inhabitants of Prussia were less German than Polish"[49].

The next discussion of population transfers came up at the Malta Conference of Foreign Ministers in February, 1945. For the first time the idea of transferring the German population from territory to be ceded to Poland was discussed. U.S. Secretary of State Stettinius was not opposed to "limited population transfers" as long as they "would not be carried out in too precipitate a fashion"[50]. Most important, Stettinius emphasized that *no* transfers were to take place before a peace treaty had been signed[51]. In the agreed minutes of the Conference Mr. Matthews was quoted as stressing that when the transfers eventually took place, they "should be gradual and not precipitate", a view shared by British Foreign Minister Eden[52]. Mr. Eden added that "the cessions upon which we and the Americans are agreed (East Prussia, Upper Silesia, Danzig and eastern Pomerania) would involve the transfer of some 2.5 million Germans. The Oder frontier, without Breslau and Stettin would involve a further 2.5 millions. The western Neisse frontier with Breslau and Stettin would involve an additional 3.25 millions making 8 millions in all"[53]. The attitude of the Western Powers was clearly against the transfer of such a large number of Germans, and the great number of Germans in territories claimed by Poland was a major factor in the Western Allies' opposition to the transfer of the Territories.

Interestingly, the issue of population transfers was not even mentioned at the Yalta Conference in February, 1945. This indicates that the Allies (at least the United States and Britain) did not consider it a pressing

matter at the time, as no transfers were contemplated until after a peace treaty had been signed to settle the territorial questions. Because territorial questions were not to be settled until the peace conference (see above), the matter of removing any populations must have been considered even more remote an issue. This explains why the Western Allies were completely caught off guard when in April reports began to come in of massive numbers of German civilians fleeing West, many having suffered severe mistreatment along the way. On April 8th the U.S. sent protests to the Russians and Poles regarding the expulsion and mistreatment of the German population in the east[54]. On April 18th Soviet Assistant Commissar for Foreign Affairs Vyshinsky replied:

> It is well known that the German population of Silesia is leaving with the withdrawing German troops and that only the Polish population remains behind. The greater part of the German civilian population has also evacuated from Danzig to Germany. In these circumstances the urgent necessity of a base for the creation of a civil administration from Poles who constitute the basic population of above mentioned areas. The direction of civil affairs in Silesia and Danzig has also been transformed to the competence of this Polish civil administration, all of which has no relation to the question of boundaries.[55]

When the entire population of Danzig was expelled at the beginning of May the United States sent another formal complaint to the Soviet Union, stating:

> The Government of the United States wishes to make it clear that the free city of Danzig and occupied German territory now subject to Polish administration as well as all other enemy territory held by the Red Army, remain in fact enemy territory under Soviet military occupation and must be held as such pending the conclusion of...agreements...between Allied powers concerned.[56]

Because of these and other strong complaints from the West, and possibly to make for a more amicable setting at the upcoming Potsdam Conference, the Soviets and Poles temporarily ceased the expulsions in June, although Germans who had previously fled were forbidden to return home[57].

The Potsdam Conference opened in July, 1945 and on July 21st the issue of the German population in territories to be annexed by Poland was first discussed. Churchill brought up the prior expulsion of German residents in some districts and the expressed intent of the Poles and Russians to expel more. He stated that "these vast transfers of population

constituted a great shock to his country", and that such movements were not good for Poland[58]. Most important, he announced: "If it was true that the Germans have run away, *they should be encouraged to come back*"[59]! Furthermore, "Poland which owes all to the Great Powers has no right to bring about a catastrophe"[60]. If at this time the British and Americans were encouraging the Germans who had fled the Oder-Neisse Territories to return to their homes, they could not have contemplated or intended their expulsion in the foreseeable future.

On July 25th the issue was again raised. Mr. Churchill argued that the German population should not be expelled from Poland proper until agreement had been reached by the Great Powers on how to properly transfer, house and feed the refugees. He added that the Germans already expelled were becoming a burden on the U.S. and British Zones of Occupation[61]. President Truman fully concurred with Churchill on this matter. They were both emphatic in their objection to the Poles expelling Germans in the Oder-Neisse Territories, considered by them to be part of the Soviet Zone of Occupation. Truman said that he would hold the Russians strictly accountable for improper actions taken by the Poles in the Occupation Zone[62].

On July 31st the draft article of the Potsdam Declaration pertaining to the transfer of German minorities was finally agreed upon. Foreign Minister Molotov stated that the article was designed to make the transfers orderly and humane, implying that the expulsions contemplated by the Big Three had not yet begun. Secretary of State Byrnes told Molotov that day that the article was acceptable, and added that "it is our information that in some cases Germans have been forced to leave". He demanded that necessary actions should be taken to prevent expulsions, at least by the Poles if not by other governments, until the proper time as set forth by the Potsdam Agreement[63]. Thus even as the second round of wholesale expulsions commenced in the Oder-Neisse Territories the Allied Powers were agreeing on a method for the *eventual* transfer of some Germans from areas to be designated Polish territory in a peace treaty.

The Potsdam Declaration issued on August 2nd contained one article pertaining to the expulsions. It reads in full:

> Article XIII: Orderly Transfer of German Populations
>
> The Conference reached the following agreement on the removal of Germans from Poland, Czechoslavakia and Hungary: The Three Governments, having considered the question in all its aspects; recognize that the transfer to Germany of German populations, or elements thereof, remaining in Poland, Czechoslavakia and Hungary, will have to be

undertaken. They agree that any transfers that take place should be effected in an orderly and humane manner.

Since the influx of a large number of Germans into Germany would increase the burden already resting on the occupying authorities, they consider that the Allied Control Council in Germany should in the first instance examine the problem with special regard to the question of the equitable distribution of those Germans among the several zones of occupation. They are accordingly instructing their respective representatives on the Control Council to report to their Governments as soon as possible the extent to which such persons have already entered Germany from Poland, Czechoslavakia and Hungary, and to submit an estimate of the time and rate at which further transfers could be carried out, having regard to the present situation in Germany.

The Czechoslavak Government, the Polish Provisional Government and the Control Council in Hungary are at the same time being informed of the above, and are being requested meanwhile to suspend further expulsions pending the examination by the Governments concerned of the report from their representatives on the Control Council.[64]

The details of these "orderly and humane transfers" contemplated by the Allies were not worked out until November, 1945 when the Berlin Protocol of the Allied Control Council set forth "practical details of the transfer and the distribution of expelled Germans"[65]. By then mass expulsions from the Oder-Neisse Territories had been underway for almost four months since the conclusion of the Potsdam Conference, plus three months prior to Potsdam, with absolutely no hint of Allied agreement or acquiescence. Not only were the expulsions carried out before the time that they were supposed to be undertaken, namely after a peace settlement determined the boundaries, but the manner of expelling the Germans did not improve at all.

The concept of expulsions of any kind in this situation flies in the face of legal norms. First, we can see that the Allied Powers did not intend or agree to commence any transfer of the German population until *after* a peace treaty had established exactly what territory inhabited by these Germans would be handed over to Poland and the Soviet Union. Not only do records of wartime and Potsdam discussions indicate an intention to forego expulsions until a settlement on boundaries had been reached (see above), but the wording of the Potsdam Declaration itself addresses this intention specifically. Article XIII refers to " the transfer to *Germany* of German populations, or elements thereof, remaining in *Poland*, Czechoslavakia and Hungary..." (emphasis added)[66]. As demonstrated in previous chapters, no German territory was transfered to Poland at Potsdam, and certainly not before. The "Poland" designated in Article

XIII could only refer to Poland within her pre-1939 borders. As we noted above, a sizeable German minority existed in pre-1939 Poland, so the concern with this population transfer by the Big Three at Potsdam is logical. Also it must be noted that the Germans of Poland are addressed indistinguishably from those of Czechoslavakia and Hungary, which did not make claims to new territory. This Article merely gave license and assistance to the transfer of minorities from and by sovereign nations. It could not apply to occupied German territory. This would also seem to fall in line with both legal and humanitarian norms. Most scholars agree that a sovereign state may, under some circumstances, expel residents from its territory. However, "what was hardly feasible or for that matter justifiable in the light of humanitarian principles was a transfer of populations other than minorities"[67], i.e. the German majority in the Oder-Neisse Territories.

Polish protagonists emphasize that at Potsdam and previous conferences there was a definite intention to transfer some German territory to Poland, and the German population of this territory would obviously be included in an article dealing with expulsion of the German minority in Poland[68]. That this is not the meaning of Article XIII is clear from the records of the conference, noted above, where discussions revolved around "*eventual* transfers" to be undertaken after the boundary question had been settled at a peace conference. Once again, the fact that no peace treaty was signed, and thus no boundary settlement was made, and thus no territory was transfered inevitably leads to the conclusion that the expulsions were an unequivocal violation of the Potsdam Accords.

The expulsions were not merely a violation of the letter and spirit of a contemporary Allied agreement. As early as 1907 the civilized nations signed the Hague Convention Respecting the Laws and Customs of War on Land[69], which specifically prohibits the removal of the civilian population in occupied territories[70]. Such removals are not prohibited when conducted pursuant to a treaty of peace at the conclusion of hostilities, conducted in a state's own territory, and done in an orderly and humane manner. In fact, a precedent for the expulsion of minority populations took place at the conclusion of World War One. Large numbers of ethnic Turks resided in areas recently annexed by Greece, pursuant to treaties concluding the two Balkan Wars of 1912 and 1913, and the late World War. Likewise, a great number of Greeks had resided in Asiatic Turkey since ancient times. Both Greece and Turkey, as well as the Allied Powers, felt that tensions in the area would be greatly reduced if these respective minorities were traded, to create homogenous nations in Turkey and Greece[71]. In fact, Harry Hopkins noted in 1945 that

President Roosevelt had been in favor of a similar transfer of populations for the Germans:

> The President said he thought we should make some arrangements to move the Prussians out of East Prussia the same way the Greeks were moved out of Turkey after the last war; while this is a harsh procedure, it is the only way to maintain peace and that, in any circumstances, the Prussians cannot be trusted.[72]

Winston Churchill agreed to "population exchanges" based upon the Greek-Turkish experience. In 1944 he stated in a speech before the House of Commons that:

> A clean sweep will be made. I am not alarmed by the prospect of the disentanglement of populations, nor even by these large transferences, which are more possible in modern conditions than they ever were before.
>
> The disentanglement of populations which took place between Greece and Turkey after the last war - my noble Friend opposite may remember - was in many ways a success, and has produced friendly relations between Greece and Turkey ever since....[73]

The model of population transfers on which these statesmen based their high hopes was sanctioned by the Treaty of Lausanne, signed with Turkey in 1923[74]. Article II called for the "orderly and humane disentanglement" of Greek and Turkish populations from the other's territory, to be overseen by the Allied Powers. There was some opposition to the principle of mass population transfers even at Lausanne, voiced mainly by British Foreign Minister Lord Curzon[75]. Indeed, even as Churchill gave his speech in the House of Commons some twenty-three years later, the Lord Bishop of Chichester denounced the idea of population transfers in the House of Lords, stating:

> There was a Turco-Greek exchange of populations after the first world war which made perhaps the best of a bad job; but it was not a model of either humanity or wisdom, and its repercussions, economic and political, are still with us. Only just over 1,000,000 Greeks were transferred from Turkish territory and, as Sir John Hope-Simpson, who was intimately concerned, has remarked, it involved an appalling amount of misery and hardship.[76]

The Lausanne transfers are easily distinguishable from the German expulsions of later times, and thus offer no precendent for them. First and foremost, the transfers were conducted pursuant to a signed and ratified

treaty between all powers concerned, including those whose peoples would be affected[77]. The German expulsions began before any type of agreement had been reached, and were concluded without any peace treaty being signed or any type of convention being concluded with the nation most affected: Germany.

Second, the territory from which each minority population was to be expelled clearly belonged to a particular nation. The Treaty of Lausanne had defined the new boundaries of Turkey[78], and all parties affected, including Turkey, signed and ratified this treaty. Thus the minorities were removed from the sovereign territory of another state, not the occupied territory of their homeland. As demonstrated above, no territorial agreement had been, or ever has been, concluded relative to the Oder-Neisse Territories, so they still retain the status of occupied German territory.

Third, the Lausanne transfers were conducted in an orderly and humane fashion, as well as could be done under the circumstances and considering the large numbers to be moved[79]. While they were far from pleasant for those involved, the governments involved did not employ a policy of systematic brutality such as that propogated by the Soviet Union and Poland in 1945.

Fourth, there was an even *exchange* of minorities, not, as in 1945, a unilateral expulsion by one nation which threw millions of destitute people onto the territory of another. Coupled with this, the persons to be exchanged were given plenty of time to pack all personal possessions, and were provided with adequate food and transportation in a reasonably orderly fashion. About two million persons were involved, but this constituted roughly an equal number moving in each direction, which minimized the economic dislocation of the countries and hardships caused by overcrowding[80]. In Germany, by contrast, over sixteen million persons were thrust upon a nation that lost virtually none to emmigration.

Lastly, and most interestingly, Articles XXX - XXXVI of the Lausanne Treaty specifically exempted from transfer Greeks and Turks inhabiting Constantinople and Western Thrace respectively who could prove that they were "established" in these territories prior to 1912, the year of the First Balkan War and radical changes of boundaries. Naturally disputes arose over who was to be exempted from transfer, and the issue was finally decided by the Permanent Court of International Justice in an advisory opinion in 1925[81]. The Court held that all persons who had maintained residence of a lasting nature in these areas, had arrived there prior to Turkey's surrender on October 30, 1918 and who had shown an intention of remaining for an indeterminate period of time were exempted from compulsory transfer[82]. Article II as interpreted by the Court made

allowance for a population which considered the transferred territory as home, and would not uproot a people who had lived and worked in the territories for centuries, or even for a few years if they contributed to its productivity. This decision was one of the first applications of a crucial new theory of international law: self-determination of peoples.

The idea of allowing a people to make its own determination of which nation it would live under was first enunciated by President Woodrow Wilson in his "Fourteen Points" in 1918. In Point Five he specified that "in determining all such questions of sovereignty the interests of the populations concerned must have equal weight with the equitable claims of the government whose title is to be determined"[83]. Still other points in the speech contained phrases such as "independent determination of her own political development" (Point Six) and "freest opportunity of autonomous development" (Point Ten). One author has noted that "eight points, all pertaining to specific territorial settlements, in common advanced the principle of self-determination"[84]. Wilson had made speeches as early as 1917 in which he said that "no peace could endure that did not foreswear any right to hand peoples about from sovereignty to sovereignty as if they were property"[85]. Three days before Wilson's "Fourteen Points" speech, Prime Minister Lloyd George made all but the first three of Wilson's points in a speech before the House of Commons[86], indicating broad support among the Western Powers for the concept of self-determination as early as the First World War.

The principle of self-determination was in fact applied in 1919 to the German minority in Poland and some German territory claimed by Poland. As for the latter, plebiscites were held in territories with mixed or majority German populations to determine whether these peoples preferred to remain part of Germany[87]. As we have seen, they voted overwhelmingly for Germany. In the case of Germans resident in Poland proper or territory annexed to Poland without plebiscite, a convention similar to that signed by Greece and Turkey relative to granting nationality to minority populations was concluded between Poland and the Allied Powers. The Permanent Court of International Justice gave an advisory interpretation of the provisions of this agreement that is almost a duplicate of its opinion concerning the Greek-Turkish agreement. The Court held that Germans now resident in Poland would be entitled to claim Polish citizenship and remain in their homes if they or their parents were habitually resident in the territories before January 10th, 1920, when the Treaty came into effect[88]. This opinion prohibited the Polish Government from denying citizenship to Germans who had formally been citizens of the German Empire, but were resident in West Prussia, Upper Silesia or Posen and now found themselves living on Polish territory. Thus the

Polish Government could not expel them as non-nationals. Furthermore, the opinion does not distinguish between former German nationals and ethnic Germans whose ancestors had inhabited central Poland for hundreds of years. They too could not be denied citizenship or expelled on account of their race. These agreements and the Court opinion alone provide ample precedent for applying the concept of self-determination to the Germans of the Oder-Neisse Territories.

The concept of self-determination was certainly not forgotten by the Allied Powers in World War Two. The second and third principles of the Atlantic Charter, issued on August 14, 1941 and adhered to by all of the Allied Powers, including Poland and the Soviet Union, specifically called for self-determination in both boundary determination and the choice of government under which a people would live[89]. Both the Soviet Union and the Lublin Poles espoused throughout the War the Leninist doctrine that all peoples have a right to self-determination, particularly that a population could separate from one country or join another as it saw fit[90]. This doctrine was enunciated by Premier Khrushchev in 1960 with regard to Third World nations, some fifteen years after the German expulsions had begun[91].

In recent times, many nations have condemned Israel for forcibly expelling Palestinians from their homeland, even though these nations recognize the State of Israel as existing on the territory of Palestine. The right to a homeland for the Palestinians does not depend upon the sovereignty of the territory, but upon an independent right to a homeland[92]. West Germany still recognizes persons born in the Oder-Neisse territories as German nationals, including those of Polish descent, and grants them entrance as citizens[93]. This application of the self-determination concept to residents of the Oder-Neisse Territories runs against the Polish interpretation of the Warsaw Treaty of 1970, which conceivably should have ended any nationality rights[94].

As the concept of self-determination had become an established principle of international law by its universal application to victors, vanquished and neutrals after World War One, and its continued enunciation through World War Two and up until the present day, the failure to apply it to the Oder-Neisse Germans violates settled international law.

The practice of states during and immediately after World War Two also indicates that the prohibition of mass involuntary expulsions had become, at the time of the German expulsions, a rule of *jus cogens* under international law. This legal norm is embodied in a number of conventions signed in the immediate post-war years, and their implementation by the signatories.

The most important of these conventions is the Convention Relative to the Protection of Civilian Persons in Time of War, signed by all major powers, including the Soviet Union and Poland, in 1949[95]. Article 49 reads in pertinent part:

> Individual or mass forcible transfers, as well as deportations of protected persons from occupied territory to the territory of the Occupying Power or to that of any other country, occupied or not, are prohibited, regardless of their motive.[96]

The Article does permit limited evacuations if necessitated for military reasons, as long as the displacement does not move persons "outside the bounds of the occupied territory"[97]. Lastly, Article 49 states that "the Occupying Power shall not deport or transfer parts of its own civilian population into the territory it occupies"[98]. The acts of the Soviet and Polish Governments in commencing the expulsions of the German population in March and April of 1945 clearly violated the wording of this Convention, as the Territories undisputably constituted occupied German territory during the closing months of the War. Furthermore, the expulsions prior to the Potsdam Conference violated these provisions, as even the Russians admitted that Germany should be considered to consist of territory within her 1937 borders, as agreed upon in the Berlin Declaration in June (see above). When the Poles and Russians began to resettle their own people on the land of the expelled German inhabitants, they once again violated Article 49.

The expulsions taking place after Potsdam, but still not sanctioned by any peace treaty or even a convention such as those signed after World War One, are invalid pursuant to Article 47 of the Civilians Convention. Article 47 reads:

> Protected persons who are in occupied territory shall not be deprived, in any case or in any manner whatsoever, of the benefits of the present Convention by any change introduced, as the result of the occupation of a territory, into the institutions or government of the said territory, nor by any agreement concluded between the authorities of the occupied territories and the Occupying Power, nor by any *annexation* by the latter of the whole or part of the occupied territory[99] (emphasis added).

According to this Article, even the claimed annexation of the Territories by Poland did not entitle the Polish Government to deprive German civilians of their property, their liberty and in many cases their lives

without a separate agreement, which the Poles and Soviets never even pretended to seek.

The principle of retaining one's homeland was also recognized in the Universal Declaration of Human Rights, issued by the United Nations in 1948 and adhered to by Poland and the Soviet Union[100]. Article 13 stands for the general principle that "everyone has the right to freedom of movement and residence within the borders of each state". The Article then goes on to read that: "everyone has the right to leave any country, including his own, *and to return to his country*" (emphasis added)[101]. Article 13 is applicable to those Germans who voluntarily fled their homes in the closing months of the War to stay away from the fighting, and then were blocked from returning to the Oder-Neisse Territories by Polish militia. Even assuming the Soviet argument that Potsdam formalized the transfer of the Oder-Neisse Territories to Poland and the Soviet Union, German civilians were kept from returning to their homes two months before the Territories had been allegedly transferred, and thus to land still indisputably German.

Detractors will argue that even though the principles for treatment of civilians clearly condemn the expulsions, these conventions do not apply to the Poles and Soviets, as they were not signed until after the War and after most of the expulsions had taken place. In refutation of this, it must be noted that there would be great hypocrisy if these conventions, signed scarcely three years after the largest expulsions took place, were not applied to their signatories for deeds that had just ended, or were still taking place. Most importantly, the conventions are mere codifications of the principles of international law already held by the signatories. No one could make an argument that in 1945 mass involuntary expulsions were acceptable in international practice, but in 1948 were universally condemned as illegal. These conventions only reinforce principles developed years before with respect to the transfer of populations. The Hague Convention of 1907, cited earlier as the first codified prohibition of expulsions in wartime, was specifically incorporated into the Civilians Convention under Article 154 of the latter[102].

Nothing, however, could more clearly demonstrate the Allies' adherence to the legal doctrine forbidding mass expulsions then their enforcement of this very principle against Germany in World War Two. As early as 1942 the Allies listed mass expulsions conducted by the Germans in eastern Europe as one of the war crimes for which the Nazi leadership would be punished after the War[103]. In 1943 the London Nine Power Act, signed by Poland, made reference to mass expulsions conducted by the Germans as a violation of the Hague Convention of 1907: "such acts of violence against the civilian population are

irreconcilable with the generally accepted principles of warfare as administered by civilized states and nations"[104]. In 1946 at the International Military Tribunal in Nurnberg, which contained one Soviet judge, Hans Frank, the Governor General of occupied Poland, was found guilty of the "crime" of ordering mass expulsions and was *executed* for this crime on October 16th[105]. Numerous other Nazi officials received severe sentences under Chapter III, Section J of the Indictment of the International Tribunal, which characterized any "forcible evacuation of the population from their homeland" as "a crime against humanity"[106]. Earlier that year, the Polish Government executed Arthur Greiser, the Gauleiter of the Warthegau, for expelling the Polish population of central Poland[107]. Apparently the Poles were unaware of the horrible irony in the fact that they had executed a man for doing exactly what they were doing at precisely the same time!

One last argument that Polish protagonists make is that even if all of the principles above hold true, and there is no doubt that they do, they would not be applicable to Germany because the Germans themselves violated these principles on numerous occasions during World War Two[108]. This "eye for an eye" principle has never been accepted in international law, or for that matter in any domestic law or statute in a civilized country. In the Treaty of Westphalia, ushering in what most consider the modern period of international law, Article V, Section 1 reads: "...quod uni parti justum est, alteri quoque sit justum"[109]. If a state condemns an act of another state as a wrong under international law, that state may not turn around and commit the same act against the first offending state simply because the first state violated the law. By the same token the mass exterminations conducted by the Nazis would not have entitled the Allies to have exterminated the entire German race after the War, although Stalin at least once mentioned this as a serious consideration. The concerns of most statesmen after the horrors of World War Two were to make sure that such horrors were never again committed by civilized nations. Certainly they would not acquiesce to a violation of this principle just because the victim had once been the victimizer. This could only lead to a vicious cycle in which the World would never be free from these wrongs.

Like the expulsions themselves, the manner in which the expulsions were conducted violated clearly set norms of international law. The Western Allies at least believed that any expulsions eventually undertaken would be done in an "orderly and humane" fashion. One writer argues that the only reason the Western Allies consented to *any* expulsions, even from sovereign states such as Czechoslavakia and Hungary, was "their sanguine belief that the transfer would be carried out in an orderly and

humane manner and that the expelling countries would co-operate with them and observe the timing and methods prescribed by the Control Council..."[110]. The Allies certainly did not approve of the brutal methods undertaken in the Oder-Neisse Territories beginning in January, 1945. The West still held to the ideals of Lausanne, improved by modern methods of transportation and planning. There was no thought of systematic abusive treatment or revenge, either before or after the end of the War, or even after a peace treaty had been signed. As Winston Churchill stated in a speech in 1944:

> the term "unconditional surrender" does not mean that the German people will be enslaved or destroyed...Unconditional surrender means that the victors have a free hand. It does not mean that they are entitled to behave in a barbarous manner...we are bound by our own consciences to civilization.[111]

Of course the brutality began even before Germany's unconditional surrender, so the Russians and Poles violated both the rules of war and the rules of peace in this instance.

The rules of international law to protect civilians from the kind of treatment received by the Germans were well established before World War Two commenced, and were set forth in the Convention Respecting the Laws and Customs of War on Land[112]. Article 23(b) forbids an enemy in time of war "to kill or wound treacherously individuals belonging to the hostile nation or army"[113]. Article 46 states that "family honour and rights, the lives of persons" must be protected, thus preventing slaughter of civilians or the breakup of their families for forced labor or internment, both of which occurred frequently in 1945-46. Article 23(d) is interesting in that it forbids a hostile power "to declare that no quarter will be given"[114]. This is directly applicable to the propaganda of Ilya Ehrenberg, which was sanctioned and published by the Soviet authorities, and called for the mass abuse and even slaughter of German civilians in furtherance of their expulsion policy.

The principles pertaining to civilian populations first enunciated at the Hague were carried forward and elaborated upon in a number of Conventions signed shortly after the War. The murder of civilians, except in cases of guerilla activity or after a fair trial, is of course strictly forbidden[115]. The Convention Relative to the Protection of Civilian Persons in Time of War forbids a state "from taking any measure of such a character as to cause..extermination of protected persons in their hands", and applies this prohibition specifically to murder[116]. Of even more importance to this aspect is the Convention on the Prevention and

Punishment of the Crime of Genocide, signed in 1948 by both Poland and the Soviet Union[117]. In this Convention the term "genocide" refers to the killing of members of a group or "deliberately inflicting on the group conditions of life calculated to bring about its physical destruction in whole or in part", and committed "with intent to destroy, in whole or in part, a national, ethnical, racial or religious group"[118]. That the intention of the Soviets and Poles was to eliminate the German population from the Oder-Neisse Territories, and in fact reduce its chances of ever populating the area again, confirms the application of the Genocide Convention to their activities in 1945-49. It is all the more applicable in that the Soviet and Polish policies in the Territories were avowedly state-supported, even encouraged. Article III of the Convention holds the following acts punishable:

> (a) Genocide; (b) Conspiracy to commit genocide; (c) Direct and public incitement to commit genocide; (d) attempt to commit genocide; (e) Complicity in genocide.[119]

Of course sections (a) and (b) are clearly applicable. Section (c) would apply to the work of Ilya Ehrenberg and others of his type. Even if Polish protagonists succeed in showing (and this is unlikely) that there was no official policy to remove or eliminate the Germans, section (e) is applicable in that the Polish authorities knew of the brutal treatment and wholesale slaughter of Germans in their villages and on their treks, and did nothing to abate it.

In like manner cruel and unusual treatment of persons, including torture, has long been forbidden, and was proscribed by the same conventions after the War. Article 27 of the Civilians Convention mandates that all protected persons should be "humanely treated, and shall be protected especially against all acts of violence or threats thereof and against insults..."[120]. Article 31 forbids "physical or moral coercion", and Article 32 prohibits a state from taking "any measure of such a character as to cause the physical suffering...of protected persons in their hands", enumerating "torture, corporal punishment, mutilation..." and related acts[121]. The Universal Declaration of Human Rights likewise prohibits subjecting people to "torture or to cruel, inhuman or degrading treatment or punishment"[122], as does the European Convention for the Protection of Human Rights and Fundamental Freedoms[123]. Poland and the Soviet Union have signed each of these conventions, yet as shown in eyewitness accounts documented above, they repeatedly and consistently violated these principles at the time the conventions were being drafted. Furthermore, at least one convention mandates that an occupying power

make adequate food and medical supplies available to the civilian population[124]. By all accounts Germans remaining in the Territories did without much food or any medical supplies for months and even years, while the Russians plundered all stocks for use in the Soviet Union.

The accounts of incidents of rape, which must have run into the millions, indicate that this was caused by more than just lax discipline on the part of Soviet authorities. It is easy to argue that such was indeed an informal policy decision. Yet the Civilians Convention specifically mandates that "women shall be especially protected against any attack on their honour, in part against rape, enforced prostitution, or any form of indecent assault"[125]. Not only did the Soviets and Poles take no action to protect innocent German women, they encouraged the rampage.

The final abuse suffered by the Germans east of the Oder-Neisse was forced labor and detention, both within the Territories and in far off reaches of Poland and Siberia. Even if we ignore the classification of this as slavery, which was abolished in the civilized world nearly one hundred years before, the principle of using forced civilian labor after the conclusion of hostilities was denounced by all of the Allied Powers in the same post-war conventions. Article 51 of the Civilians Convention prohibits an occupying power to compel protected persons to work, unless such is necessary to restore food production and public utilities, and in any case the persons must be over eighteen years old[126]. Article 51 also specifies that "the work shall be carried out only in the occupied territory where the persons whose services have been requisitioned are"[127]. The Convention calls for a fair wage to be paid to the laborers. Naturally, none of these principles were adhered to by the Soviets and Poles. Article 4 of the Universal Declaration of Human Rights[128] also prohibits involuntary servitude, as does Article 4 of the European Convention for the Protection of Human Rights and Fundamental Freedoms[129].

German military personnel who were caught in the east faired no better than civilians. The fact that most spent ten years in Siberian labor camps, and many never returned from captivity, is itself proof of violations of numerous articles of the Hague Convention of 1907[130], as well as the Convention Relative to the Treatment of Prisoners of War, signed in Geneva in 1949 by Poland and the Soviet Union[131]. What we are particularly concerned with here is the fate of "local troops" in the Territories, mainly the Volksturm, or "people's militia"[132]. The Volksturm units wore military uniforms and fought alongside regular army units. There are no accounts of their carrying on guerilla activities or spy missions after the occupation[133]. Nevertheless, there is strong evidence that captured Volksturm members were not treated as regular German

army personnel (not that this would have significantly improved their lot), and on at least one notable occasion (Königsberg) they were led to a mass execution[134]. While all of the legal provisions relating to prisoners of war should have been applied to the Volksturm, there was no support under any classification for their mass slaughter after surrender. Article 23(c) of the Hague Convention of 1907 recognizes the ancient principle of civilized nations that forbids a belligerant "to kill or wound an enemy who, having laid down his arms, or having no longer means of defence, has surrendered at discretion"[135].

Polish and Soviet protagonists will raise several defenses to the application of these conventions to their actions in the Territories. The first one, that all except the Hague Convention were signed after the War and are inapplicable, has been addressed above. However, it is also important to note that all of the violations listed above were included in the indictment of the International Military Tribunal at Nurnberg in 1945. Article 6 of the Charter of the International Military Tribunal, signed on August 8, 1945 by the Soviet Union and the Western Powers, reads in pertinent part:

> The following acts, or any of them, are crimes coming within the jurisdiction of the Tribunal for which there shall be individual responsibility:... (b) War crimes. Namely, violations of the laws or customs of war... (c) Crimes against humanity. Namely, murder, extermination, enslavement, deportation, and other inhumane acts committed against any civilian population before or during the war or persecutions on political, racial, or religious grounds in execution of or in connection with any crime within the jurisdiction of the Tribunal....[136]

Once again, it is apparent that the rules and norms codified in the post-war conventions were already recognized as *jus cogens* in 1945, when the expulsions began.

The Soviets' next argument will be that while they may be bound by the rules enunciated at Nurnberg, they can not be responsible for actions taken by the Polish authorities and population, as Poland did not participate at Nurnberg and was not a party to any agreement until after the War. In answer to this it must be remembered that Poland was a Soviet-occupied country just like Germany, from the middle of 1944 until many years after the War (in fact it is still effectively under occupation). Throughout the entire period of the expulsions Soviet authorities dominated Poland, and the Lublin Polish Government took orders directly from Moscow. Polish military, militia and civilian authorities acted as agents under orders from Russian military and civilian commands. Article

29 of the Civilians Convention states that: "The Party to the conflict in whose hands protected persons may be, is responsible for the treatment accorded to them by its agents, irrespective of any individual responsibility which may be incurred"[137]. As the Russians were in firm control throughout eastern Europe, particularly in Poland, and as the Oder-Neisse Territories were considered part of the Russian zone of occupation at least until Potsdam (see above), the Soviets would be held accountable for all of the violations committed by Polish authorities.

The Poles will also give the argument that they were entitled to implement their own policies in the Territories, before Potsdam because of wartime necessity, and after Potsdam not only because of their claim of annexation, but also because even the Western Powers had recognized their right to an occupation zone. This ignores the fact that the rights guaranteed under international law apply to all persons and territories regardless of their status. Article 2 of the Universal Declaration of Human Rights, which was adhered to by Poland, reads in part: "no distinction shall be made on the basis of the political, jurisdictional or international status of the country or territory to which a person belongs..."[138]. When a norm of international law becomes a rule of *jus cogens*, as those enumerated above have, the fact that a state has not become a party to a specific convention recording that norm makes no difference in its applicability to the activities of that state.

Our last consideration is the status of the property of the expellees, most of which was seized prior to or during the expulsions. The Hague Convention of 1907 forbids a belligerent "to destroy or seize the enemy's property, unless such destruction or seizure be imperatively demanded by the necessities of war"[139]. In the same Convention "pillage" is specifically forbidden in two articles, even when a town is taken by assault[140]. The private property of individuals, as well as municipalities, is protected from seizure in *all* cases, the only exceptions being cash, funds and securities belonging *solely* to the state, and depots of arms[141]. Likewise, the post-War Civilians Convention holds that "any destruction by the Occupying Power of real or personal property belonging individually or collectively to private persons, or to the State, or to other authorities, or to social or cooperative organizations, is prohibited, except where destruction is rendered absolutely necesary by military operations"[142]. Pillage of any sort is also proscribed[143]. These conventions alone would seem to condemn both the pillage undertaken by arriving Russian and Polish troops in 1944-45, and the later seizure of real and personal property by Polish and Russian authorities when expelling the German inhabitants, and by Polish militia and other authorities while the Germans were on their treks.

In all wars there will be a certain amount of hooliganism on the part of conquering armies, especially when their countries have suffered a similar fate earlier in the war. What is most reprehensible in the Oder-Neisse situation is the loss of all property, even personal valuables, by the German population during the "organized" expulsions. Even the Greek and Turkish populations moved pursuant to the Lausanne Treaty were allowed to take personal property with them. Most important, because the Oder-Neisse Territories had not been handed over to Poland and Russia by treaty, and were still considered occupied territory pending a peace treaty, not only the expulsions but the property seizures were invalid. The Permanent Court of International Justice addressed this issue specifically after World War One, when German territory was validly transferred by treaty to Poland[144]. In twin cases, the Court addressed issues pertaining to property rights in Upper Silesian territory transferred to Poland after a peace treaty and plebiscite had determined the territory's status. The Polish Government seized all German property in the area[145], but also refused to recognize property sales and rights acquired under German law after Germany's surrender on November 11th, 1918. The territory was not formally transferred to Poland until 1923. The Court held that until the time that the status of Upper Silesia had been formally determined and the territory formally annexed by Poland all German property rights, including the right to transfer property under German law, should be respected. Therefore Polish acts of non-recognition and retroactive seizures were invalid[146]. In another decision issued two years earlier, the Permanent Court of International Justice held with respect to German nationals in the provinces of Posen and West Prussia, now part of Poland, that they were entitled to retain their personal property as well as assume Polish nationality[147]. Applying these Court opinions to the Oder-Neisse problem, it becomes clear that no property should have been seized, much less any German nationals expelled, prior to the formal transfer of territory after a peace treaty had been signed. As no such treaty was ever signed, all of the seizures and destruction carried out by the Russian and Polish authorities, and their failure to prevent Polish and Russian citizens and soldiers from looting the German homes and treks, are clear violations of international law.

In violating a number of established principles of international law with respect to the treatment of civilians and their property in occupied territory, the Polish and Soviet Governments have exposed themselves to liability and penalties, as have the individuals who carried out these acts. For a government to fall under the theory of State Liability, four factors must be met[148]. First, there must be a breach of an international obligation or rights of states. In this case numerous states rights have been violated.

Second, the fault or culpability must be due to a willful act on the part of the offending state. Certainly the acts of the Polish and Soviet authorities were willful and deliberate. Third, there must be an injury caused by the act. This is indisputable. Fourth, the act or omission causing the injury must be imputable to the state or its agents. It is clear from first-hand testimony as well as official records that the expulsions were a deliberate policy on the part of the Polish and Soviet Governments, and were planned and implemented by them through their personnel, military and bureaucratic. In the case of the Soviets this was done mainly through their Lublin Polish puppets. Last, there must be a lack of justification for the actions taken by the state. It is hard to justify the sudden mass removal of millions of people from their ancestral homelands, especially before any agreements had been reached between the occupying powers and the occupied state, or even with their own allies. It is impossible to justify the inhumane manner in which such removals were conducted, regardless of the background or circumstances.

Judging from this analysis, the Soviet and Polish Governments must be held liable for the inhumane and illegal act of expelling the German population from the Oder-Neisse Territories. Modern international law provides remedies for violations of these principles. The Civilians Convention obligates its signatories, which include Poland and the Soviet Union, to enact domestic legislation necessary to effect penal sanctions for persons committing breaches of the Convention, and furthermore requires that the signatories search for persons having committed such violations[149]. The Convention also forbids any signatory from absolving itself or any other signatory from any liability incurred under the Convention[150]. The specific acts for which a party is deamed liable and punishable under the Convention include:

> wilful killing, torture or inhuman treatment, ...unlawful deportation or transfer or unlawful confinement of a protected person, compelling a protected person to serve in the forces of a hostile Power, or wilfully depriving a protected person of rights of fair and regular trial prescribed in the present Convention...or extensive destruction and appropriation of property, not justified by military necessity and carried out unlawfully and wantonly.[151]

Under this Convention alone the Polish and Russian Governments could be brought to justice for most of the acts committed during the expulsions.

The Genocide Convention obligates a state to bring to justice any individuals who violate the provisions of the Convention. Under Article VI, "persons charged with genocide or any of the other acts enumerated in

Article III shall be tried by a competent tribunal of the State in the territory of which the act was committed, or by such international penal tribunal..."[152]. As we have seen, military and civilian officials in Poland and the Soviet Union could be brought to justice for four of the five enumerated violations in Article III. Such has been done with respect to Nazis accused of violating these norms during the War, even in West German courts. It is high time that Poland and especially the Soviet Union, in its new era of denouncing the Stalinist past, bring to justice their own people who committed crimes as heinous and illegal as those of the Nazis. They can no longer claim that their own authorities did no wrong.

With respect to the vast amount of property lost by the expellees, compensation is due. This is only logical in light of the illegal manner in which it was taken from them, and would come with the remedies enumerated above. Furthermore, the fact that the transfer of the Oder-Neisse Territories to Poland never occurred under law, and thus is a nullity, presents a firmer case for return of all property seized. When the property of a state or its citizens is taken in violation of international law it must all be returned or compensation paid, even if the taking was a mistake, and not a deliberate violation of law. The International Court of Justice confirmed this principle in the Case Concerning the Temple of Preah Vihear[153]. In that case, Cambodia and Thailand disputed the ownership of a strip of border territory which included an ancient monument and many artifacts. Thailand had occupied the site for many years and had removed some artifacts. The Court determined that the Temple and surrounding land belonged to Cambodia, and held that Thailand was obligated to return all artifacts removed from the area, even though the temple had been occupied by Thailand in good faith for over a century. The Court decided that Cambodia had never lost sovereignty over the area, and Thailand had never gained it, during the period in question. Since Poland and the Soviet Union have never obtained valid title to the Oder-Neisse Territories, they too are obligated to return all property seized, public and private.

Notes

1. Accounts of the Nemmersdorf episode abound, along with many others. See: Gunter Boddeker, *Die Fluchtlinge*, 11-25 (1980); Alfred de Zayas, *Nemesis at Potsdam* (1977).

2. Zoltan Michael Szaz, *Germany's Eastern Frontiers*, 94 (1960).

3. *Id*.

4. The best collection of first-hand accounts of the Russian occupation of eastern Germany can be found in: Theodor Schieder, *The Expulsion of the German*

Population from the Territories East of the Oder-Neisse Line, (1959). See especially 48-54. See also: Ralph F. Keeling, *Gruesome Harvest* (1947).

5. This was especially true in Gauleiter Koch's East Prussia, which lay closest to the Russian front, and had the second largest population of the east German provinces, next to Silesia. Because of this, when the final Russian offensive began many East Prussians could not escape in time. Dieckert and Grossmann, *Der Kampf um Ostpreussen* (1960).

6. Schieder, *Supra*; Keeling, *Supra*.

7. Harry Truman, *Memoirs*, Vol. I, 367 (1955). Several writers argue that the brutality of the Russian occupation troops was part of a grand design to annex the Territories. See for example: Szaz, *Supra*, at 91-94.

8. Numerous good works give detailed descriptions of the military campaigns in eastern Germany. See: Hans Schaufler, *1945 - Panzer an der Weichsel*; Hans von Ahlfen, *Der kampf um Schlesien*; Dieckert and Grossmann, *Supra*.

9. Dieckert and Grossmann, *Supra*; Boddeker, *Supra*, at 26-36, 91-109.

10. Dieckert and Grossmann, *Supra*, at 98-109.

11. Egbert Kieser, *Danziger Bucht*, (1978); Boddeker, *Supra*, at 46-58.

12. Kieser, *Supra*; Boddeker, *Supra*; Dieckert and Grossmann, *Supra*. During the evacuation many German ships loaded with refugees were sunk by Russian submarines and airplanes. The greatest passenger vessel disaster in history occurred during this time. On January 30th the German luxury liner *Wilhelm Gustloff* was sailing from the Bay of Danzig to northern Germany with 6040 evacuees and wounded soldiers when she was torpedoed by a Russian submarine. Over 5100 persons perished, more than on the *Titanic* and the *Lusitania* combined! Dobson, Miller and Payne, *Die Versenkung der "Wilhelm Gustloff"* (1979).

13. Schieder, *Supra*, at 62.

14. Already in March the Poles began to divide up German territory under their control into *voivodes*, or administrative districts, to conform with the Polish system. Elizabeth Wiskemann, *Germany's Eastern Neighbors* (1956).

15. Most of the information on the fate of the German inhabitants after the Russian occupation can be found in: Schieder, *Supra* and Bodekker, *Supra*. The author has heard personal accounts from many East Prussians now resident in West Germany.

16. Otto Lasch, *So Fiel Königsberg* (1984).

17. The most complete collection of first-hand accounts is found in: Johannes Kaps (ed.), *The Tragedy of Silesia, 1945-46* (1952); see also: Keeling, *Supra*.

18. A first hand account of the terrible suffering of the people of Silesia was related to the author by a German maid who worked for the author's family. In 1945 she was still living in her home town of Oppeln, in eastern Silesia. Her family refused to flee before Russian troops overran her town in January. The soldiers that occupied her town were Mongolian, from Soviet Central Asia. To them a German woman was no better than a dog or horse. Their comportment she described as "barbaric, non-human". The raping and looting went on for days, and many persons were shot for no apparent reason, at the whim of the drunken Soviet soldiers. A few days later German troops managed to temporarily retake the town, and she and her sister were evacuated. They were forced to hike west in the dead of winter, on foot with only a small cart loaded with belongings, as transport was

very scarce. At the end of January they arrived in Dresden, which was packed with refugees. While our maid wanted to remain in Dresden and rest, her sister insisted on moving further west. Two days later the city of Dresden was firebombed by the British and an untold number of women and children who had fled to the apparant safety of Dresden were incinerated. Our maid attributed her survival to divine countenance. I would attribute anybody's survival in those days to divine countenance.

19. Von Ahlfen and Niehoff, *So Kampfte Breslau* (1984). This was one of the most heroic battles of the campaign for the Oder-Neisse Territories. At the same time the fanatical Nazi authorities in Breslau treated the population almost as badly as the Russians, shooting anyone even suspected of shirking his duty. What remained of the city's population was almost immediately expelled after the surrender.

20. Friedrich von Wilpert, *The Oder-Neisse Problem*, 80 (1969).

21. Most of the accounts of the post-war expulsions come from: Schieder, *Supra*; Szaz, *Supra* at 125-131; Alfred M. de Zayas, *Supra*, at 6-13; Boddeker, *Supra*.

22. See: De Zayas, *Supra*; Keeling, *Supra*.

23. Even Pope Pious XII denounced this "repugnant and unacceptable" act. Hans Schoenberg, *Germans from the East*, 22 (1970).

24. The best account of the Germans' living conditions in the Territories from 1945 to 1947 is: Hans Graf von Lehndorff, *Ostpreussisches Tagebuch* (1961). This is the diary of a doctor and member of one of East Prussia's most prominent families, who travelled through East Prussia during the years 1945-47 and noted the terrible conditions that had befallen his homeland. For a detailed account of Polish expulsion policy and Western reaction, see: Szaz, *Supra*, at 125-131.

25. See: Hugo Linck, *Königsberg 1945-1948* (1952). The conditions of the German population of Königsberg were improved during their last year there, and a small German society was reestablished among the now predominantly Russian population of the City. However, in 1948 every last German was expelled to the West. A few Königsbergers, mostly children, managed to escape to Lithuania and still reside there.

26. Vilius Peteraitis, "Mazosios Lietuvos Vietovardziu Svetimejimas XX Amziuje", *Lithuania Minor*, 251-73 (1976). While the Poles could use the indigenous names of many towns and places in eastern Germany that had once been partially or wholly Polish, there had never been a Russian culture in East Prussia, and all of the Russianized names came from unrelated regions of the Soviet Union, as did the settlers. In later years Lithuanians were allowed to repopulate part of this area, and now make up about the same percentage of the population as they did before the War. See: Helmut Peitsch, *Wir Kommen aus Königsberg: Nord-Ostpreussen Heute* (1979). Lithuanians do of course make up most of the population of the Memel Territory, which was given to the Lithuanian S.S.R. in 1946. No expulsions were ever undertaken in Memel, and presumably a substantial German minority, probably bilingual, still resides there.

27. Kaps, *Supra*; Szaz, *Supra* at 130. Between 1955 and 1959 the Polish Government instituted a "reuniting of families" program, which allowed the first large emigration of Germans to the West since the expulsions. After this the Poles claimed that no more Germans were living in the Territories, but several more

migrations occurred in later years. Many of these persons were probably Germans who had been held as prisoners or forced laborers in Poland and the Soviet Union. See: Z. Anthony Kruszewski, *The Oder-Neisse Boundary and Poland's Modernization*, 15-17 (1972). Kruszewski gives much lower figures for the number of Germans expelled after the end of the War and the number remaining in the Territories. He believes both that most Germans fled during the War and did not return, and that after the "reuniting of families" campaign few if any Germans remained east of the Oder-Neisse. His book was published before the 1980s migrations.

28. Charles Wassermann, *Europe's Forgotten Territories* (1960).

29. P. Ruge, *Nicht nur die Steine Sprechen Deutsch...* (1985); Stephan M. Horak, *Eastern European National Minorities, 1919-1980*, 55 (1985).

30. Amity Shlaes, "East Bloc Germans Invade Germany", *The Wall Street Journal*, July 28, 1988. The author personally met some ethnic Germans living in southern East Prussia when he travelled there in 1985. Many of the young have intermarried with Poles, so in most cases only the older Germans retain their language, although in many instances the Poles will adopt German customs and food. A few villages remain wholly German.

31. G.C. Paikert, *The German Exodus*, 8 (1962).

32. Federal Ministry for Expellees, *Facts Concerning the Problem of the German Expellees and Refugees*, Appendix (1952).

33. De Zayas, *Supra* XXV; Federal Ministry, *Supra*, Appendix.

34. Joanne E. Holler, *The German Expellees: A Problem of Integration*, 6 (1963). The Oder-Neisse Provinces, being farthest away from Allied air bases, were considered the "bomb shelter of Germany", and many Germans evacuated to them after Allied air raids began in earnest in 1943. It is thus impossible to know exactly how many persons were actually living in the Territories in the Spring of 1945.

35. German Federal Republic, *Statistical Pocket-Book on Expellees* (1953).

36. De Zayas, *Supra*. Some sources put this casualty figure much higher. See: Federal Ministry, *Supra*, Appendix.

37. Gerhard Reichling, *Die Heimatvertriebenen im Spiegel der Statistik*, 14-15 (1958). These figures add up to more than the estimate of those expelled. This is because the former includes those expellees arriving before the end of the War.

38. Paiket, *Supra*, at 78.

39. Theodor Schieder (ed.), *The Expulsion of the German Population from Czechoslavakia* (1960). Some 267,000 Germans died in this expulsion, and approximately 250,000 remained in Czechoslavakia. De Zayas, *Supra*.

40. Federal Ministry, *Supra*. For accounts of the typical brutal treatment during these expulsions, see: Theodor Schieder, *The Fate of the Germans in Hungary and the Fate of the Germans in Rumania* (1960).Rough estimates indicate that 1,294,000 Germans remained in these areas after the expulsions. Federal Ministry, *Supra*.

41. Reichling, *Supra*, at 15.

42. See: Schoenberg, *Supra*.

43. Federal Ministry, *Supra*, Appendix. The expulsions also caused economic problems in Poland, for much agricultural land went fallow for many years, and underproduction in the Territories made Poland a net importer of food as well.

Woclaw Sobanski, *Western and Northern Territories of Poland: Demographic Problems* (1959); Goettinger Research Committee, *The German Eastern Territories in Light of the Polish Press* (1958); Peter-Heinz Seraphim, "Die Wirtschaft Ostdeutschlands", *Die Deutschen Ostgebiete* (1952).

44. Whiteman, "German-Polish Frontier" *Digest of International Law* Vol.3, 284 (1960).

45. Federal Ministry, *Supra* Annex; German Federal Republic, *Supra*. Many of these Germans had been residents of the German Empire before the provinces of Posen and West Prussia and part of Silesia were handed to Poland by the Treaty of Versailles in 1919. Others were descendants of German settlers who had been invited into Poland by the medieval Piast Dynasty to build the Polish kingdom. See: Norman Davies, *God's Playground: A History of Poland*, Vol. I, 61-105 (1982). Interestingly, by 1950 only 410,000 German expellees from Poland were living in West Germany, and an indeterminate number in East Germany. This indicates that while the post-1939 settlers from the Third Reich were immediately expelled, most of the true Polish-Germans were probably allowed to stay, either because they were bilingual or because they were needed to rebuild "their" country.

46. Schoenberg, *Supra*.

47. Whiteman, *Supra*, at 294 (emphasis added).

48. *Id*.

49. Holborn, *War and Peace Aims of the United Nations*, 1080 (1948).

50. Wiskemann, *Supra*, at 83.

51. *Id*.

52. Whiteman, *Supra*, at 295.

53. Whiteman, *Supra* at 296.

54. Heinz G. Sassa, "The Prelude to the Expulsions and Oder-Neisse Line from 1939-1945" *Eastern Germany*, Vol.II, 412 (1963).

55. Whiteman, *Supra*, at 301.

56. Sassa, *Supra*, at 413.

57. See above. This was certainly done to boost Stalin's argument that there was no problem with annexing vast tracts of German territory, as the population had already fled, not necessitating large transfers.

58. Whiteman, *Supra* at 320.

59. *Id*. Emphasis added.

60. *Id*. Churchill was especially concerned about the loss of food supplies for Germany should the great farmlands of the Oder-Neisse Territories not be available to the Germans.

61. Whiteman, *Supra*, at 331; see also: Charles Mee, Jr. *Meeting at Potsdam* (1975).

62. Whiteman, *Supra* at 332.

63. Whiteman, *Supra*, at 340; Mee, *Supra*. The discussions at Potsdam seemed to make little distinction between the Polish expulsions in Poland proper and the Oder-Neisse Territories, or for that matter between those conducted by the Polish Administration and those conducted by the Governments of Hungary, Czechoslavakia and other countries. This may indicate that the Western Allies did not believe that German residents were being expelled from what was still considered occupied German territory. Their concern may have been directed at making the transfer of Germans from other countries, which arguably is more

legitimate, as humane as possible. The issue of expulsions from other sovereign countries gives rise to a distinct set of legal issues, and is beyond the scope of this work.

64. Mee, *Supra* Appendix II.

65. Z. Jordan, *Oder-Neisse Line*, 15 (1952).

66. Mee, *Supra*, Appendix II.

67. de Zayas, *Supra*, at 9.

68. Benno Zundorf, *Die Ostvertrage*, 63 (1979).

69. 36 Stat. 2277, T.S. No.539, 205 C.T.S. 295 (Oct. 18, 1907).

70. *Id*., Article XLIV.

71. For an overview of this population trade, see: Demetrios Pentzopoulos, *The Balkan Exchange of Minorities and its Impact upon Greece*, (1962).

72. Cordell Hull, *The Memoirs of Cordell Hull*, 1265 (1948).

73. *Parliamentary Debates*, House of Commons, 15 December 1944, Vol. 406, col. 1484.

74. *Treaty of Lausanne*, 28 L.T.S. 11 (July 24, 1923). The Lausanne Treaty incorporated by reference and implication the *Convention on the Exchange of Greek and Turkish Populations* (Exchange Convention), 32 L.T.S. 75 (January 30, 1923) signed by Greece and Turkey.

75. Henry Morgenthau, *I Was Sent to Athens* (1929); De Zayas, *Supra*, at 11.

76. *Parliamentary Debates*, House of Lords, Vol. 139, col. 68, 30 January 1946.

77 The actual agreement relating to the transfers was: *Convention on the Exchange of Greek and Turkish Populations*, 32 L.T.S. 75 (Jan. 30, 1923). This was incorporated into the Treaty of Lausanne in several articles, including Article XIV.

78. *Treaty of Lausanne*, *Supra*, Articles II - XV.

79. There was considerable suffering on the part of both Turks and Greeks in their transfers, including removal from ancestral homelands, the loss of lands and houses, and even in some cases looting and physical abuse by authorities of the other nationality. However, the official policy, which both Governments as well as the Allied Powers tried to enforce, was to ameliorate hardships as well as possible, and provide compensation in the form of land and provisions for both peoples upon their arrival in the other country. See: Pentzopoulos, *Supra*; Morgenthau, *Supra*.

80. Inis L. Claude, *National Minorities*, 94 (1955).

81. *Exchange of Greek and Turkish Populations* (Advisory Opinion), 2 P.C.I.J. Ser.B, No.10 (1925).

82. 1 P.C.I.J. ser.B, No.10, at 25-26.

83. The "Fourteen Points" were part of a speech given by President Wilson before Congress on January 8, 1918. They are reprinted in: Laurence W. Martin, *Peace Without Victory*, Appendix (1958).

84. John Martin Blum, *Woodrow Wilson and the Politics of Morality*, 148 (1956).

85. Martin, *Supra*, at 125.

86. Blum, *Supra*, at 148.

87. See historical summary chapter, above. A plebiscite was also held in Schleswig-Holstein, which led to its division between Denmark and Germany. The only territories where plebiscites were not held were in Posen, West Prussia and the Memelland in the east, and Alsace-Lorraine and Eupen and Malmedy in the

west. Even in the latter many statesmen wished to apply a plebiscite, but Wilson thought that leaving Alsace-Lorraine with Germany, even if a plebiscite result gave a clear preference for Germany, would cause more trouble for the peace of Europe than it would be worth to follow the preferences of the small population concerned. See: Blum, *Supra*.

88. *The Question Concerning the Acquisition of Polish Nationality* (Advisory Opinion), 2 P.C.I.J. Ser. B, No.7 (1923).

89. Reprinted in: De Zayas, *Supra*, Appendix.

90. Herbert Kraus, *The Status Under International Law of the Eastern Territories of Germany*, 98 (1963).

91. *Id*.

92. Fritz Munch, "Die Rechtsstellung der Deutschen Ostgebiete", *Internationales Recht und Diplomatie* 29, 30 (1970).

93. This has led to considerable complaints in West Germany. Massive numbers of ethnic Poles have emigrated to West Germany in search of better jobs and been granted residence as German nationals due to their place of birth in the Oder-Neisse Territories.

94. See: Otto Kimminich, "Der Warschauer Vertrag und die Staatsangehorigkeit der 'Polen-Deutschen'", 24 *Die Offentliche Verwaltung* 577 (Sept., 1971).

95. *Convention Relative to the Protection of Civilian Persons in Time of War*, August 12, 1949. 75 U.N.T.S. 287, 6 U.S.T. 3516.

96. *Id*, Article 49.

97. *Id*.

98. *Id*.

99. *Id*., Article 47.

100. *Universal Declaration of Human Rights*, Dec. 10, 1948, U.N.G.A. Res. 217A (III), U.N. Doc. A/810, at 71 (1948).

101. *Id*.

102. 75 U.N.T.S. 287, Article 154. The 1899 Hague Convention is also incorporated.

103. Claude, *Supra*, at 102.

104. Paikert, *Supra*, at 44, n.2. The Soviet Union did not sign this Declaration.

105. Paikert, *Supra*, at 45, n.1.

106. *Id*.

107. *Id*.

108. See generally: Paikert, *Supra*, at 15-16; Kraus, *Supra*, at 99-100.

109. "what is righteous for one party must also be righteous for the other one". *Peace Treaty of Westphalia*, 1 C.T.S. (Oct. 14, 1648), Article V, Section 1. n.2.

110. De Zayas, *Supra*, at 12.

111. 397 H.C. Deb. (5th ser.) cols. 698-699 (Feb. 22, 1944).

112. 36 Stat. 2277, T.S. No.539, 205 C.T.S. 295 (1907).

113. *Supra*., Art.23.

114. *Supra*., Art. 23(d).

115. *European Convention for the Protection of Human Rights and Fundamental Freedoms*, Europ. T.S. No.5 (Nov. 4, 1950), Article 2.

116. 75 U.N.T.S. 287, 6 U.S.T. 3516 (August 12, 1949), Article 32. Cited hereafter as "Civilians Convention".

117. 78 U.N.T.S. 277 (Dec. 9, 1948). Cited hereafter as "Genocide Convention".

118. *Supra*., Art. II.

119. *Id*.

120. 75 U.N.T.S. 287, Article 27.

121. *Supra*, Articles 31 and 32.

122. U.N.G.A. Res. 217 A (III), U.N. Doc. A/810, at 71 (1948), Article 5.

123. *European Convention*, *Supra*, Art.3.

124. *Civilians Convention*, 75 U.N.T.S. 287, Art. 55.

125. *Supra*, Article 27.

126. *Supra*., Article 51.

127. *Id*.

128. *Supra*, Article 4.

129. Europ. T.S. No.5 (Nov. 4, 1950). Article 70 of the Civilians Convention also prohibits detention of individuals for acts committed or opinions expressed before the occupation, except for breaches of the laws and customs of war. Certainly all nine or ten million German residents of the Territories were not war criminals.

130. See particularly Articles 4-19. 205 C.T.S. 205.

131. 6 U.S.T. 3316, 75 U.N.T.S. 135 (Aug. 12, 1949). Articles 12-120.

132. These were militia units raised in the last year of the war in German territory near the front, and were composed mostly of old men and boys as young as twelve years old. When regular uniforms were not available they were issued with clearly distinguishable arm bands, and carried an assortment of military-issue weapons and equipment. Considering the terrible state of supply of the German Army on the Eastern Front in 1944-45, the Volksturm really did not look too much different than their Wehrmacht comrades.

133. There had been plans laid by the more fanatical Nazis to employ the "Werewolves" to carry on a guerilla war after Germany's surrender. Except for a few isolated incidents, mainly in western Germany, this idea never came to fruition.

134. See above.

135. *Supra*, Article 23(c).

136. *Charter of the International Military Tribunal*, August 8, 1945, reprinted in: Ian Brownlie, *Principles of Public International Law*, 561 (1979).

137. *Supra*, Article 29.

138. *Supra*, Article 2.

139. 36 Stat. 2277, T.S. No. 539, 205 C.T.S. 295, Article 23(g).

140. *Supra*, Articles 28 and 47.

141. *Supra*, Articles 46, 53 and 56.

142. 75 U.N.T.S. 287, Article 53.

143. *Supra*., Article 33.

144. *Case Concerning Certain German Interests in Polish Upper Silesia* (Germany v. Poland). 1 P.C.I.J. Ser. A, No.7 (1926); *Case Concerning Certain German Interests in Polish Upper Silesia* (Germany v. Poland). 1 P.C.I.J. Ser. A, No.6 (1925).

145. The value of such property was accredited to Germany's war reparations.

146. *Id*.

147. *Certain Questions Relating to Settlers of German Origin in the Territory Ceded by Germany to Poland* (Advisory Opinion). 2 P.C.I.J. Ser.B, No.6 (1923). 106

148. Information on the Doctrine of State Liability was obtained from a lecture given by Professor Bernard Oxman at the University of Miami School of Law in October, 1986.

149. 75 U.N.T.S. 287, Article 146.

150. *Supra*, Article 148.

151. *Supra*, Article 147.

152. 78 U.N.T.S. 277, Article VI.

153. *Case Concerning the Temple of Preah Vihear* (Cambodia v. Thailand). (1962) I.C.J. 6.

6

CONCLUSION

It is indisputable that neither the Potsdam Accords nor any other wartime agreement, treaty or conference created a cession, valid under international law, of the Oder-Neisse Territories to Poland. The Allied Powers did not conclude the requisite peace treaty with Germany that would transfer the territory, and never came to an agreement on exactly what territory to transfer. Subsequent events, including the Gorlitz Agreement, have no impact on this situation. As of 1970 the Oder-Neisse Territories remained under the sovereignty of Germany. When the German population in this area was expelled and their property seized this was a gross violation not only of the right of self-determination, but also of Germany's sovereign right over her territory. This is to say nothing of the violations of international law caused by the inhumane manner of the expulsions.

Contrary to much current thought, the Treaties of Warsaw and Moscow in 1970 did not change the legal status of the Oder-Neisse Territories, which remain legally a part of Germany. These treaties, by admission of the signatories, did not create a legal cession, but merely confirmed a supposedly existing cession. However, that "existing cession" could never have occurred. Furthermore, the German entity party to the treaties, as with the Gorlitz Agreement, did not have the standing to conclude any such agreement. Finally, the 1970 Treaties and the Helsinki Accord relating to the inviolability of frontiers are mere non-aggression agreements, and the ultimate disposition of the Oder-Neisse Territories, if any, remains for a future peace conference concluded with and signed by a united Germany, as direct successor to the old Reich.

What this boils down to is that even now, forty-four years after the end of World War Two, Poland and the Soviet Union are illegally in

occupation of territory that belongs to Germany. Both the German Nation and the ten million Germans expelled from this area were terribly wronged. Even more ominous, the continued support or tacit acceptance of this situation by many statesmen, jurists, scholars and governments sets a precedent for future military conquests, unilateral annexations and mass expulsions. By failing to denounce the current situation and take action to correct it, they give validity to a condition that contradicts modern treaties and universally accepted legal concepts.

Countless writers have addressed some aspect of the Oder-Neisse Problem over the years, but few have really suggested any solution. Today with the stalemate in central Europe between East and West most any solution, however simple, would be near impossible. By "solution" we mean a just solution, not recognition or acquiescence in a boundary wrongfully formed, even if this wrong took place a half century ago. Only when a unified German state, the reconstituted German Reich, is formed can a treaty of peace be negotiated to settle properly all of the issues arising out of World War Two. Thus reunification of Germany is the preliminary goal. This could be accomplished by forming a cordon of non-aligned states through the heart of Europe, with a reunified German state as the center of this band of neutrals. With a neutral Germany there would be less fear of negotiating a fair peace, and the non-aligned cordon separating East and West would ease tensions throughout the region.

The Oder-Neisse Territories could then be returned to Germany. Immediate transfer of administration to Germany should be followed by careful resettlement policies, with the utmost care to prevent any hardship for the Poles presently living in these lands. Some adjustments in the frontiers would be made to leave historically Polish areas within Poland, but all such judgments should be based upon the situation prior to the forced expulsions of the War years. Of course Poles and their descendants moved into the Territories after 1945 would have to be transferred back to Poland as Germans are resettled on their native lands, but they should be both humanely treated and compensated for their hardship. As for the German expellees and their families, the Soviet and Polish Governments should be brought before the International Court of Justice and ordered to pay compensation to private individuals. These Governments should also be compelled to restore to Germany all property plundered or purposely damaged during and after the War, or pay appropriate compensation.

This writer is not so naive as to believe that the scenario outlined above will take place in the near future. We must therefore conclude on the negative note that the Oder-Neisse Line will remain a blemish on the map of Europe as the greatest travesty of justice in modern international law.

However, this situation can have an immediate affect on state practice by serving as a warning to prevent such a situation from ever happening again. We can not allow any state, be it fighting for right or wrong, to take unilateral actions in the annexation of territory, or the expulsion of a population, that are so repugnant to basic norms of international law and common decency. To allow the Polish and Russian Governments to go unchallenged for these violations, even so many years later, is reprehensible. The Charter of the German Expellees expresses this ideal most succinctly:

> We have lost our homeland. The homeless are strangers on the face of the earth. Almighty God himself placed men in their native land. To separate a man from his native land by force means to kill his soul. We have suffered and experienced this fate. We, therefore, feel competent to demand that the right to our native land be recognized and be realized, as one of the basic rights of man, granted to him by the grace of God...The nations must realize that the fate of the German expellees, just as that of all refugees, is a world problem, the solution of which calls for the highest sense of moral responsibility and the stern necessity of making a tremendous effort....[1]

Notes

1. Excerpted from: *Charter of the German Expellees*, signed in Stuttgart on August 5, 1950. Reprinted in: Friedrich von Wilpert, *The Oder-Neisse Problem*, Appendix (1969).

BIBLIOGRAPHY

BOOKS

von Ahlfen and Niehoff. *So Kampfte Breslau*. Stuttgart: Motorbuch Verlag, 1984.

von Ahlfen, Hans. *Der Kampf um Schlesien*. 1960.

Association of Expellee-Landsmannschaften. *The European Significance of the Oder-Neisse Territories*. Goettingen: Goettingen Arbeitskreis, 1956.

Blum, John M. *Woodrow Wilson and the Politics of Morality*.
Boston: Little, Brown and Co., 1956.

Boddeker, Gunter. *Die Fluchtlinge*. Munchen: F.A. Herbig Verlagsbuchhandlung, 1980.

Bradley, John. *Czechoslovakia*. Edinburgh: University Press, 1971.

Brownlie, Ian. *Principles of Public International Law*. Oxford: Clarendon Press, 1979.

Brownlie, Ian. *African Boundaries: A Legal and Diplomatic Encyclopaedia*. Oxford: Clarendon Press, 1979.

Carsten, Francis. *The Origins of Prussia*. Westport, Conn: Greenwood Press, 1981.

Church, Alfred and William Brodribb (trans.). *The Agricola and Germany of Tacitus*. London: Macmillan and Co., 1911.

Churchill, Winston S. *Closing the Ring*. Boston: Houghton Mifflin Co., 1951.

Churchill, Winston S. *Triumph and Tragedy*. Boston: Houghton Mifflin Co., 1953.

Claude, Inis L. *National Minorities*. New York: Greenwood Press, 1969.

Czarnecki, Jan. *The Goths in Ancient Poland*. Coral Gables: University of Miami Press, 1975.

Daniel, Glyn. *The Balts*. 1963.

Davies, Norman. *God's Playground: A History of Poland* (Two Vol.) Vol.I. New York: Columbia University Press, 1982.

Deutsches Volkerrechts Verein. *Worterbuch des Volkerrechts*. Vol.I 1960.

Dieckert and Grossmann. *Der kampf um Ostpreussen*. Stuttgart: Motorbuch Verlag, 1985.

Dobson, Miller, Payne. *Die Versenkung der "Wilhelm Gustloff"*. Munchen: Wilhelm Heyne Verlag, 1979.

Drzewieniecki, W.M. *The German-Polish Frontier.* Chicago: Polish Western Association of America, 1959.

Dvornik, Francis. *The Slavs in European History and Civilization*. New Brunswick, N.J: Rutgers University Press, 1962.

Eversley, George. *The Partitions of Poland*. New York: Howard Fertig, 1973.

Farley, Lawrence T. *Plebiscites and Sovereignty*. Boulder: Westview Press, 1986.

Fay, Sidney. *The Rise of Brandenburg-Prussia to 1786*. New York: Henry Holt and Co., 1937.

Federal Ministry for Expellees, *Facts Concerning the Problem of the German Expellees and Refugees*. 1952.

Feis, Herbert. *Between War and Peace*. Princeton: Princeton University Press, 1960.

Gause, Fritz. *Geschichte des Preussenlandes*. Leer: Verlag Gerhard Rautenberg, 1966.

Gayre, G.R. *Teuton and Slav on the Polish Frontier.* London: Eyre and Spottiswoode, 1944.

German Federal Republic. *The Treaty of August 12, 1970*. Press and Information Office, 1970.

German Federal Republic. *Statistical Pocket-Book on Expellees*. Wiesbaden: Federal Statistical Office, 1953.

Gerutas, Albertas. *Lithuania: 700 Years*. New York: Manyland Books, 1984.

Gimbutas, Marija. *The Balts*. London: Thames and Hudson, 1963.

Goettinger Research Committee. *The German Eastern Territories in Light of the Polish Press*. Wuerzburg: Holzner, 1958.

Goudy, A.P. "Racial Origins", *The Cambridge History of Poland*. (W.F. Reddaway, et.al., ed.) Cambridge: The University Press, 1950.

Grant, Michael. *Ancient History Atlas*. London: Weidenfeld and Nicolson, 1981.

Griffith, William E. *The Ostpolitik of the Federal Republic of Germany*. Cambridge, Mass: The M.I.T. Press, 1978.

Halecki, Oscar. *Borderlands of Western Civilization*. New York: The Ronald Press Co., 1952.

Heiss, Friedrich. *Deutschland und der Korridor*. Berlin: Volk und Reich Verlag, 1939.

Holborn, Louise W. (ed.) *War and Peace Aims of the United Nations*, 2 Vol. Boston: World Peace Foundation, 1948, Vol.II.

Holler, Joanne E. *The German Expellees: A Problem of Integration*. Washington: George Washington University Press, 1963.

Horak, Stephan M. *Eastern European National Minorities, 1919-1980*. Littleton, Colorado: Libraries Unlimited, 1985.

Hull, Cordell. *The Memoirs of Cordell Hull*. New York: The Macmillan Co., 1948.

Jordan, Z. *Oder-Neisse Line*. London: Polish Freedom Movement, 1952.

Jurgela, Constantine. *History of the Lithuanian Nation*. New York: Lithuanian Cultural Institute, 1948.

Jurgela, Constantine. *Lithuania: The Outpost of Freedom*. New York:

Kaiser, Karl. "The New Ostpolitik", *West German Foreign Policy: 1949-1979* (Hanreider, ed.). 1980.

Kann, Robert A. *A History of the Habsburg Empire 1526-1918*. Berkeley: University of California Press, 1977.

Kaps, Johannes (ed.). *The Tragedy of Silesia, 1945-46*. Munchen: Christ Unterwegs, 1952.

Keeling, Ralph F. *Gruesome Harvest*. Chicago: Institute of American Economics, 1947.

Kertesz, Stephen D. *The Last European Peace Conference: Paris 1946-Conflict of Values*. Lanham, Md: University Press of America, 1985.

Kieser, Egbert. *Danziger Bucht 1945*. Munchen: Wilhelm Heyne Verlag, 1978.

Kmietowicz, Frank. *Ancient Slavs*. Stevens Point, Wis: Worzalla Publishing Co., 1976.

Koch, H.W. *A History of Prussia*. London: Longman Group, 1978.

Korey, William. *Human Rights and the Helsinki Accord*. New York: Foreign Policy Association, 1984.

Kraus. *Die Oder-Neisse Linie*. Koln-Braunsfeld, 1954.

Kraus. *The Status Under International Law of the Eastern Territories of Germany within the Frontiers of the Reich as at 31st December, 1937*. Gottingen, 1963.

Krollmann, Christian. *The Teutonic Order in Prussia*. Elbing: Preussen-Verlag, 1938.

Kruszewski, Z. Anthony. *The Oder-Neisse Boundary and Poland's Modernization*. New York: Praeger Publishers, 1972.

Lasch, Otto. *So Fiel Königsberg*. Stuttgart: Motorbuch Verlag, 1984.

Laubert, Manfred. *Nationalitat und Volkswille*. Breslau: Ferdinand Hirt, 1925.

von Leers, Johann. *Memelland*. Munchen: Verlag Frz. Eher Nachf., 1932.

Graf von Lehndorff, Hans. *Ostpreussisches Tagebuch*. Munchen: Biederstein Verlag, 1961.

Linck, Hugo. *Königsberg 1945-1948*. Leer: Verlag Gerhard Rautenberg, 1952.

Maleczynskiego, Karola. *Historia Slaska*. Wroclaw: Instytut Historii Polskiej Akademii Nauk, 1961.

Martin, Laurence W. *Peace Without Victory*. New Haven: Yale University Press, 1958.

Mee, Charles L. *Meeting at Potsdam*. New York: M. Evans and Co., 1975.

Morgenthau, Henry. *I Was Sent to Athens*. Garden City, N.J: Doubleday, Doran and Co., 1929.

Ortmayer. *Conflict, Compromise and Conciliation: West German-Polish Normalisation 1966-1976*. Denver: University of Denver, 1975.

Pagel, Karl. *The German East*. Berlin: Konrad Lemmer Verlag, 1954.

Paikert, G.C. *The German Exodus*. The Hague: Matinus Nijhoff, 1962.

Peitsch, Helmut. *Wir Kommen aus Königsberg*. Leer: Verlag Gerhard Rautenberg, 1980.

Pentzopoulos, Demetrios. *The Balkan Exchange of Minorities and its Impact upon Greece*. Paris: Mouton and Co., 1962.

Peteraitis, Vilius. "Mazosios Lietuvos Vietovardziu Svetimejimas XX Amziuje", *Lithuania Minor* (Martin Brakas, ed.). New York: Lithuanian Research Institute, 1976.

Pounds, Norman. *Eastern Europe*. Chicago: Aldine Publishing Co., 1969.

Pounds, Norman. *The Upper Silesian Industrial Region*. Bloomington,Ind: Indiana University Press, 1958.

Reichling, Gerhard. *Die Heimatvertriebenen im Spiegel der Statistik*. Berlin: Verlag von Duncker & Humblot, 1958.

Rhode, Gotthold. *Die Ostgebiete des Deutschen Reiches*. Wurzburg: Holzner Verlag, 1956.

Rosenthal, Harry K. *German and Pole*. Gainsville: University Presses of Florida, 1976.

Ruge, E. and P. *Nicht nur die Steine sprechen deutsch...* Munchen: Langen Muller, 1985.

Sasse, Heinz Gunther. "The Prelude to the Expulsions and Oder-Neisse Line from 1939-1945", *Eastern Germany, Two Vol.* Wuerzburg: Holzner Verlag, 1963 (Vol. II).

Scharloff, Willi. *Königsberg-Damals und Heute*. Leer: Verlag Gerhard Rautenberg, 1982.

Schaufler, Hans. *1945 - Panzer an der Weichsel*. 1965.

Schieder, Theodor. *The Expulsion of the German Population from the Territories East of the Oder-Neisse Line*. Bonn: Federal Ministry for Expellees, Refugees and War Victims, 1959.

Schieder, Theodor. *The Fate of the Germans in Hungary and the Fate of the Germans in Rumania*. Bonn: Federal Ministry for Expellees, Refugees and War Victims, 1960.

Schieder, Theodor. *The Expulsion of the German Population from Czechoslavakia*. Bonn: Federal Ministry for Expellees, Refugees, and War Victims, 1960.

Schmalstieg, William. *Studies in Old Prussian*. University Park, Pa: Pennsylvania State University Press, 1976.

Schoenberg. *Germans from the East*. The Hague, 1970.

Schutz, Herbert. *The Prehistory of Germanic Europe*. New Haven: Yale University Press, 1983.

Schwarz. "Adenauer's Ostpolitik", *West German Foreign Policy: 1949-1979* (Hanreider, ed.). Boulder: Westview Press, 1980.

Seraphim, Peter-Heinz. "Die Wirtschaft Ostdeutschlands", *Die Deutschen Ostgebiete*. Stuttgart: Brentano-Verlag, 1952.

Sharma, Surya P. *International Boundary Disputes and International Law*. Bombay: N.M. Tripathi Private, 1976.

Sobanski, Waclaw. *Western and Northern Territories of Poland, Demographic Problems*. Poznan: Wydawnictwo Zachodnie, 1959.

Stettinius, Edward R. *Roosevelt and the Russians*. Garden City, N.Y: Doubleday and Co., 1949.
Stiklorius, Jonas A. "Lithuania Minor in International Treaties", *Lithuania Minor* (Martin Brakas, ed.). New York: Lithuanian Research Institute, 1976.
Szaz, Zoltan M. *Germany's Eastern Frontiers*. Chicago: Henry Regnery Co., 1960.

Terry, Sarah M. *Poland's Place in Europe*. Princeton: Princeton University Press, 1983.
Tims, Richard W. *Germanizing Prussian Poland*. New York: A.M.S. Press, 1966.
Treitske, Heinrich G. *Origins of Prussianism*. New York: Howard Fertig, 1969.
Truman, Harry. *Memoirs* Vol. I. Garden City, N.J: Doubleday & Co., 1955.

Wambaugh, Sarah. *Plebiscites Since the World War*, Two Vol. Washington: Carnegie Endowment for International Peace, 1933. Vol. I.
Wassermann, Charles. *Europe's Forgotten Territories*. Copenhagen: R. Roussell, 1960.
Watt, Richard M. *The King's Depart*. New York; Simon and Shuster, 1968.
Weis, P. *Nationality and Statelessness in International Law*. Westport, Conn: Hyperion Press, 1979.
Whetten. *Germany's Ostpolitik*. London: Oxford University Press, 1971.
Wiewiora, Boleslaw. *Polish-German Frontier from the Standpoint of International Law*. Poznan: Wydawnictwo Zachodnie, 1959.
von Wilpert, Friedrich. *The Oder-Neisse Problem*. New York: Edition Atlantic-Forum, 1969.
Wiskemann, Elizabeth. *Germany's Eastern Neighbors*. London: Oxford University Press, 1956.

de Zayas, Alfred M. *Nemesis at Potsdam*. London: Routledge and Kegan Paul, 1977.
Zundorf, Benno. *Die Ostvertrage*. Munchen: Verlag C.H. Beck, 1979.

ARTICLES

Albert, "Bonn's Moscow Treaty and Its Implications." *International Affairs*, Vol.47 (April, 1971).
Arndt, "Rechtliche und politische Aspekte der deutschen Ostpolitik." *Osterreichische Zietschrift fur Aussenpolitik*, Vol.14 (1974).
Arndt, "Legal Problems of the German Eastern Territories." *American Journal of International Law*, Vol.74 (Jan., 1980).
Arndt, "Zu einigen Rechtsproblemen der deutsch-polnischen Vereinbarungen von 1975." *Zeitschrift fur Recht und Politik*, Vol.13 (1977-78).

Berezowski, "Zagadnienie granicy polsko-niemieckiej w swietle radzieckiego projektu traktatu pokoju z Niemcami." ("Problem of the Polish-German Boundary in light of the Soviet Treaty with Germany") *Panstwo i Prawo,* Vol.14 (Nov., 1959).

Bognar, "Politicko-Geografske i Geopoliticke Osobine Granica Poljske." *Jugoslovenska Revija za Mesunarodno Pravo*, Vol.19 (1972).

Briggs, "The Leader's Agreement - Yalta." *The American Journal of International Law*, Vol.40 (1946).

Dunin-Keplicz, "Poland and the Two Germanys." *Afro-Asian and World Affairs*, Vol.3 (19).

Fifield, "The Postwar World Map: New States and Boundary Changes." *The American Political Science Review*, Vol.42 (1948).

Frowein, "Legal Problems of the German Ostpolitik." *International and Comparative Law Quarterly*, Vol.26 (Jan., 1974).

Gelberg, "The Warsaw Treaty of 1970 and the Western Boundary of Poland." *American Journal of International Law*, Vol.76 (Jan., 1982).

Gelberg, "The Case of the Treaty Concerning the Bases of Relations between the GDR and the FRG." *Polish Western Affairs*, Vol.15 (1974).

Janicki, "Legal Problems Involved in the Realization by the Federal Republic of Germany of the Treaty with Poland Dated 7th December, 1970." *Polish Western Affairs*, Vol.18 (1977).

Janicki, "The Territory and State Citizenship in the Legal Systems of the German Democratic Republic and the German Federal Republic." *Polish Western Affairs*, Vol.12 (1971).

Jasica, "The Legislation of the Federal Republic of Germany and the Problem of Normalization of Mutual Relations between the Polish People's Republic and the Federal Republic of Germany." *Polish Yearbook of International Law*, Vol.7 (1975).

Jasudowicz, "The Prohibition to Apply the *rebus sic stantibus* Norm with Respect to Treaties Establishing National Frontiers." *Polish Yearbook of International Law*, Vol.8 (1976).

Johnson, D.H.N. "Acquisitive Prescription in International Law." *British Yearbook of International Law*, Vol.27 (1950).

Kaikobad, "Some Observations on the Doctrine of Continuity and Finality of Boundaries." *British Yearbook of International Law*, Vol.54 (1982).

Kelsen, Hans. "The Legal Status of Germany According to the Declaration of Berlin." *American Journal of International Law*, Vol. 39 (1945).

Kimminich, "Die Ostvertrage." *Internationales Recht und Diplomatie*, Jahrbuch (1971).

Kimminich, "Der Warschauer Vertrag und die Staatsangehorigkeit der 'Polen-Deutschen'." *Die Offentliche Verwaltung*, Vol.24 (Sept., 1971).

Klafkowski, "The Forms of Recognition of State Frontiers after the Second World War." *Jahrbuch fur Ostrecht*, Vol.5 (May, 1964).

Libera, "Prawno-miedzynarodowe uznanie suwerennosci Polski nad Ziemiami Zachodnimi." ("International Recognition of Poland's Sovereignty over Her Western Territories"). *Panstwo i Prawo*, Vol.18 (Jan., 1963).

MacGibbon, I.C. "The Scope of Acquiescence in International Law." *British Yearbook of International Law*, Vol. 31 (1954).

Mann, F.A. "Germany's Present Legal Status Revisited." *International and Comparative Law Quarterly*, Vol.16 (July, 1967).

Mann, F.A. "The Present legal Status of Germany." *International Law Quarterly*, Vol.1 (1947).

Mattern, "The Employment of the Plebiscite in the Determination of Sovereignty." *Johns Hopkins University Studies in Historical and Political Science*, Vol.38 (1920).

Menon, P.K. "International Boundaries-A Case Study of the Guyana-Surinam Boundary." *International and Comparative Law Quarterly*, Vol.27 (Oct., 1978).

Meyer-Lindenberg, "Deutschlands Grenzen, Die Aussage des Volker-rechts." *Internationales Recht und Diplomatie*, (1964).

Molodtsov, "Peaceful Settlement of Territorial Disputes and Frontier Issues." *Sovetskii Ezhegodnik Mezhdunarodnogo Prava*, (1963).

Munch, "Die Rechtsstellung der Deutschen Ostgebiete." *Internationales Recht und Diplomatie*, (1970).

Oka, "Warming trend sets in for Soviet-Japanese ties." *Christian Science Monitor*, (October 25, 1988).

Oppermann, "Das Ende der Bundesrepublik Deutschland? Die verfassungspolitische Perspektive der Ostvertrage." *Internationales Recht und Diplomatie*, Jahrbuch (1972).

Pan, "Legal Aspects of the Yalta Agreement." *The American Journal of International Law*, Vol.46 (1952).

Poeggel, "Deutschlands Grenzen - Die Aussage des Volkerrechts." *Staat und Recht*, Vol.13 (March, 1964).

"Prussians." *Encyclopedia Lituanica*, (1982).

Rosenthal, "The Assimilation and Integration of the German Expellees." *Polish Review*, Vol.8 (Winter, 1963).

Schmidt, Helmut. "Germany in the Era of Negotiations." *Foreign Affairs*, Vol. 49 (Oct., 1970).

Sharp, "The Russian Annexation of the Königsberg Area, 1941-1945." *Survey*, Vol.23, No.105 (Autumn, 1977).

Shlaes, "East Bloc Germans Invade Germany." *The Wall Street Journal*, (July 28, 1988).

Skubiszewski, "Les traites sur les frontieres en Europe centrale (1970-1973)." *Polish Yearbook of International Law*, Vol.6 (1974).

Skubiszewski, "Poland's Western Frontier and the 1970 Treaties." *American Journal of International Law*, Vol.67 (Jan., 1973).

Skubiszewski, "Nowe traktaty w sprawach niemieckich: problemy terytorialne." ("New Treaties on German Affairs"). *Panstwo i Prawo*, Vol.28 (May, 1973).

Skubiszewski, "Zachodnia granica Polski w swietle ukladow z 1970 roku." ("The Western Frontier of Poland and the 1970 Treaty"). *Panstwo i Prawo*, Vol.26 (March-April, 1971).

Skubiszewski, "The Great Powers and the Settlement in Central Europe." *Jahrbuch fur Internationales Recht*, Vol.18 (1975).

Staar, "The Polish-German Boundary: A Case Study in International Law." *Journal of Public Law*, Vol.11 (Spring, 1962).

Steinberger, "Volkerrechtliche Aspekte des deutsch-sowjetischen Vertragswerks vom 12. August 1970." *Zeitschrift fur Auslandisches Offentliches Recht und Volkerrecht*, Vol.31 (1971).

Subbarao, "Polish Case for the Oder-Neisse Frontier: A Juridical View." *The Indian Journal of International Law*, Vol.9 (1969).

Symonides, "The Inviolability of Frontiers and the Territorial Integrity in the Treaties between Poland and the GDR, between Poland and the FRG, and in the Final Act of the Helsinki Conference." *Polish Yearbook of International Law*, Vol.11 (1981-1982).

Thompson, "East German Colonization in the Middle Ages." *Annual Report of the American Historical Association for the Year 1915*, (1917).

Tyranowski, "State Succession: Boundaries and Boundary Treaties." *Polish Yearbook of International Law*, Vol.10 (1979-1980).

Weissberg, "Review of Arndt's 'Die Vertrage von Moskau und Warschau'." *The American Journal of International Law*, Vol.71 (1978).

Whiteman, "German-Polish Frontier." *Digest of International Law*, Vol.3 (1963).

Whiteman, "Territory and Sovereignty of States." *Digest of International Law*, Vol.2 (1963).

Whiteman, "Civilian Aliens." *Digest of International Law*, Vol.10 (1963).

Wiewiora, "Zachodnioniemieckie roszczenia terytorialne wobec Polski a prawo miedzynarodowe." ("West German Territorial Claims Against Poland in Light of International Law"). *Panstwo i Prawo*, Vol.15 (Dec., 1960).

Wiewiora, "West German Territorial Claims Against Poland and International Law." *Polish Western Affairs*, Vol.2 (1961).

Woolsey, "The Polish Boundary Question." *American Journal of International Law*, Vol.38 (1944).

Wright, "Poland and the Crimea Conference." *American Journal of International Law*, Vol.39 (1945).

Yanovsky, "The German Peace Treaty and the Oder-Neisse Border." *Sovetskii Ezhegodnik Mezhdunarodnogo Prava*, (1962).

Zieger, "Das neue Gesetz uber die Staatsgrenze der DDR." *Recht in Ost und West*, Vol.27 (Jan., 1983).

TREATIES AND CONVENTIONS

Agreement Between the Polish Republic and the German Democratic Republic Concerning the Demarcation of the Established and Existing Polish-German State Frontier, July 6, 1950 (Gorlitz or Zgorzelec Treaty). 1959 U.N.T.S. 104.

Instrument Confirming the Demarcation of the State Frontier between Poland and Germany, January 27, 1951 (Frankfurt Instrument). 1959 U.N.T.S. 110.

Treaty between the Federal Republic of Germany and the Union of Soviet Socialist Republics, August 12, 1970 (Moscow Treaty). 9 I.L.M. 1026.

Treaty between the Federal Republic of Germany and the People's Republic of Poland Concerning the Basis for Normalization of Their Mutual Relations, December 7, 1970 (Warsaw Treaty). 10 I.L.M. 127, 1972 U.N.T.S. 332.

Treaty between the Polish People's Republic and the German Democratic Republic Concerning the Delimitation of the Continental Shelf in the Baltic Sea, October 29, 1968. 1971 U.N.T.S. 260.

Treaty on the Basis of Intra-German Relations, December 21, 1973. 12 I.L.M. 16.

Treaty Between the Polish Republic and the Union of Soviet Socialist Republics Concerning the Polish-Soviet State Frontier, August 16, 1945. 10 U.N.T.S. 193.

Agreement Between the Government of the Polish Republic and the Government of the Union of Soviet Socialist Republics Concerning the Regime on the Soviet-Polish State Frontier, July 8, 1948. 37 U.N.T.S. 25.

Treaty Between the United States, the British Empire, France, Italy and Japan and Associated Powers and Germany, June 28, 1919 (Treaty of Versailles). 225 C.T.S. 189.

Final Act of the Conference on Security and Cooperation in Europe, August 1, 1975 (Helsinki Accords). Reprinted in: Kavass, Igor, Jacqueline Granier and Mary Dominick, *Human Rights, European Politics, and the Helsinki Accord: The Documentary Evolution of the Conference on Security and Co-operation in Europe 1973-1975*. Buffalo, N.Y: William S. Hein & Co., 1981.

Treaty Between Austria-Hungary, France, Germany, Great Britain, Italy, Russia and Turkey for the Settlement of Affairs in the East, (Berlin Treaty), July 13, 1878. 153 C.T.S. 171.

Vienna Convention on the Law of Treaties (Vienna Convention), May 22, 1969. 8 I.L.M. 679.

Convention on the Prevention and Punishment of the Crime of Genocide, (Genocide Convention), December 9, 1948. 78 U.N.T.S. 277.

Convention Between the United Kingdom, the United States, France and the Federal Republic of Germany on Relations Between the Three Powers and the Federal Republic of Germany (Three Power Agreement), May 26, 1952. 331 U.N.T.S. 328.

Treaty Concerning Relations Between the Union of Soviet Socialist Republics and the German Democratic Republic, Sept. 20, 1955. 226 U.N.T.S. 208.

Convention on Succession of States in Respect of Treaties (Vienna Treaty Convention), August 13, 1978. Doc. A/CONF. 80/31.

Peace Treaty of Lausanne, July 24, 1923. 28 L.T.S. 11.

Convention on the Exchange of Greek and Turkish Populations, January 30, 1923. 32 L.T.S. 75.

Peace Treaty of Westphalia, October 14, 1648. 1 C.T.S. 246.

Universal Declaration of Human Rights, December 10, 1948. U.N.G.A. Res. 217A (III), U.N. Doc. A/810, at 71 (1948).

European Convention for the Protection of Human Rights and Fundamental Freedoms, November 4, 1950. Europ. T.S. No.5.

Charter of the International Military Tribunal, Nurnberg, August 8, 1945.

Convention Relative to the Treatment of Prisoners of War, August 12, 1949. 6 U.S.T. 3316, 75 U.N.T.S. 135.

Hague Convention Respecting the Laws and Customs of War on Land, October 18, 1907. 36 Stat. 2277, T.S. No. 539, 205 C.T.S. 295.

Convention Relative to the Protection of Civilian Persons in Time of War (Civilians Convention), August 12, 1949. 75 U.N.T.S. 287, 6 U.S.T. 3516.

CASES AND LAWS

Case Concerning Certain German Interests in Polish Upper Silesia (Germany v. Poland). 1 P.C.I.J. Ser.A, No.6 (1925).

Case Concerning Certain German Interests in Polish Upper Silesia (Germany v. Poland). 1 P.C.I.J. Ser.A, No.7 (1926).

Exchange of Greek and Turkish Populations (Advisory Opinion). 2 P.C.I.J. Ser.B, No.10 (1925).

Interpretation of the Statute of the Memel Territory (Advisory Opinion). 6 P.C.I.J. Ser.A/B, No.49 (1932).

Certain Questions Relating to Settlers of German Origin in the Territory Ceded by Germany to Poland (Advisory Opinion). 2 P.C.I.J. Ser.B, No.6 (1923).

The Question Concerning the Acquisition of Polish Nationality (Advisory Opinion). 2 P.C.I.J. Ser.B, No.7 (1923).

Legal Status of Eastern Greenland (Norway v. Denmark). 6 P.C.I.J. Ser. A/B, No.53 (1933).

Island of Palmas Case (United States v. The Netherlands). 22 A.J. 867 (1928).

Lighthouses in Crete and Samos. P.C.I.J. ser. A/B, no. 71 (1937).

Case Concerning the Temple of Preah Vihear (Cambodia v. Thailand), (1962) I.C.J. 6.

Case Concerning Sovereignty over Certain Frontier Land (Belgium v. Netherlands). (1959) I.C.J. 209.

Interpretation of Peace Treaties with Bulgaria, Hungary and Romania (Advisory Opinion). (1950) I.C.J. 65.

R. v. Bottrill ex parte Kuechenmeister. (1946) 1 All E.R. 635.

Basic Law of the Federal Republic of Germany (Grundgesetz), as amended August 23, 1976.

SPEECHES, PAPERS AND OTHER DOCUMENTS

The Bahr Paper, May 22, 1970. Reprinted in: Whetten, *Germany's Ostpolitik* (1971).

Speech by British Foreign Secretary Anthony Eden before the House of Commons. 397 H.C. Deb. No.35, May 24, 1944.

Speech by Representative Carrol Reece "On German Provinces East of the Oder-Neisse Line, and Economic, Historical, Legal and Political Aspects Involved, Congressional Record, Vol.103, Part 6 (1957).

Speech by Mr. Fitzroy McLean before the House of Commons. 484 H.C. Deb., Col. 1271, Feb. 20, 1951.

Speech by Prime Minister Winston Churchill before the House of Commons. Parliamentary Debates, House of Commons, 15 December 1944, Vol. 406, col. 1484.

Speech by Prime Minister Winston Churchill before the House of Commons. 397 H.C. Deb. (5th ser.), cols. 698-699 (February 22, 1944).

Speech by the Lord Bishop of Chichester before the House of Lords. Parliamentary Debates, House of Lords, Vol. 139, col. 68, 30 January 1946.

Bühler, Phillip. *The Rape of Central Europe: The Oder-Neisse Line and the Amputation of Eastern Germany, 1941-1950.* (1983), (Available at the College of William and Mary Department of Government Library, and from the author).

INDEX